MANNERS WILL TAKE YOU PLACES MONEY WON'T:

*My Journey from the Backwoods
of Georgia to the Rainforests of West Africa*

By
CASHAWN MYERS

Copyright © 2025 by Cashawn Myers. All rights reserved. No part of this publication may be reproduced, distributed, or transmitted in any form or by any means, including photocopying, recording, or other electronic or mechanical methods, without the prior written permission of the author or publisher, except in the case of brief quotations embodied in critical reviews and certain other noncommercial uses as permitted by U.S. copyright law.

For permission requests, contact Cashawn Myers at cashawnmyers@gmail.com. Silver Bangles Productions books may be purchased for educational, business, or sales promotional use at www.silverbanglesproductions.com. For more information, please email info@silverbanglesproductions.com.

Interviews and transcriptions provided by Sheree Swann

Book Cover by 52 Design Studio

Book Cover Photo by Sheree Swann

Printed in Atlanta, GA, U.S.A.

First printing, December 2025

Library of Congress Cataloging-in-Publication Data is available on file

ISBN: 979-8-9888463-5-2

This book is dedicated to every person who has poured into me as a child and those who continue to pour into me as an adult.

FOREWORD

I cannot remember the moment that I met Ras Cashawn Myers. Our brotherhood was forged in the late 90s in the fire that was known as the Washington D.C. Nyahbinghi House. At the time, we were both students at Howard University and members of a large group of Howard students and grassroots young adults who had embraced Ras Tafari. It was during this era that we made the decision to give our lives in service of H.I.M. Emperor Haile Selassie I and African liberation and redemption. We quickly became close brethren and would go on to become founding members of Howard University's first Ras Tafari student organization, The Ethiopian Ras Tafari Community (E.R.C.).

Over the years, we have done countless works together, and I feel honored to call Ras Cashawn one of my closest brethren. I have witnessed Ras Cashawn's tireless work ethic and have celebrated his victories as he achieved many milestones. From building and maintaining a beautiful family with his chosen queen, Shevon Myers, to the founding of H.A.B.E.S.H.A. Inc., to the groundbreaking establishment of K.A.S.I., Ras Cashawn has blazed a trail that will be studied by generations of pan-Africanists.

This book will mark another historic milestone. It is the lion telling his own story. It also represents the children of Ras Tafari following the footsteps of H.I.M. Emperor Haile Selassie I and not waiting for others to tell their story or ascribe value to their works. Just as Haile Selassie I took time during his exile in England in 1936, Ras Cashawn has taken the time in his 50th year to document his journey from rural Georgia to Ghana, West Africa. In light of the magnitude of his achievements, this book should be required reading for Ras Tafari and Pan African youth and serve as a guiding light for those who choose to walk the narrow path to repatriation, African liberation, and the ultimate unification of the African continent.

-Kwasi O. Bonsu, Esq.

TABLE OF CONTENTS

PREFACE 9

PLAYLIST 11

CHAPTER 1: *Divine Timing* 13

CHAPTER 2: *Planted in Fertile Soil* 19

CHAPTER 3: *Transformation* 33

CHAPTER 4: *Cultivation* 47

CHAPTER 5: *Expansion* 75

CHAPTER 6: *Fruition* 83

CHAPTER 7: *Succession* 95

CONCLUSION 103

ACKNOWLEDGEMENTS 105

ABOUT THE AUTHOR 107

PREFACE

My story is ordinary in some ways and uncommon in others. But this book isn't being told because of me; it's being told because of the people who have shaped me. Their lessons, their sacrifices, and their love made me the man I am. Some now walk in the ancestral realm while others still walk beside me, and I carry them all. This is your story, told through me. I give thanks.

***

My story began on December 15, 1975, in Brunswick, Georgia, at Glynn County Hospital, when my mother, Rita—known to many as Mama Rita—brought me earthside at just fifteen years old. Many people assumed that her story would end there, or that mine would only get so far. They couldn't have been more wrong.

For years, people have told me I should write a book. Now, as I approach my half-century mark, the timing finally feels divine. My truth doesn't stand alone; it's woven with the wisdom and guidance of those who came before me and those who walk beside me now.

Tarshia has known me from the very beginning. Though she's my cousin, she's always felt more like an older sister. As she puts it, *"Shawn was the person who dreamed big, but it was never just about him. It was bigger than him; it was always gonna be about success for the community, something to build culture-wise."*

I grew up steeped in family and familiar with the power and true meaning of legacy. Growing up in a small community, practically everyone was family. Because my mother had me young, my grandparents played a huge role in my life. The elders in the community saw me as their own grandson. I knew dirt roads, cow pies, wild blueberries, swimming holes, and sitting at my grandmother's feet before I ever understood city life and the world around me.

This book is for anyone who comes from a line of strong people and still had to learn how to be strong for themselves—for the ones navigating identity, legacy, and healing, not just for their own sake but for the ones who couldn't. My life has unfolded in many phases, but themes like identity, service, inheritance, and spiritual guidance have remained steady. In this book, you'll hear from elders, family, peers, and people whose stories mirror my own in ways I never expected. My great-grandma Susie used to say, "*Manners will take you places money won't.*" I hope the stories in this book do something similar—carry you where only love, truth, and spirit can.

This isn't a typical memoir. I'm sharing my story not only for myself and future generations, but to honor the people who shaped me. These pages hold my experiences, but they also hold the voices of my community, my family, my village—because my life has never been lived alone.

We live in a world where our bodies, voices, and histories are questioned, distorted, or erased. Telling our stories becomes an act of protection and power. This is me claiming my own narrative and refusing to let anyone else define it. My life has never been a solo journey, and I won't allow it to be remembered as one.

PLAYLIST

CHAPTER 1
Luther Vandross - *"Bad Boy / Having a Party"* - 1982
Newcleus - *"Jam On It"* - 1984
RUN DMC - *"My Adidas"* - 1986

CHAPTER 2
The Pharcyde - "Passin' Me By" - 1992
Eightball & MJG - "Pimps" - 1993
Outkast - "Players Ball" - 1994

CHAPTER 3
Goodie Mob - "Cell Therapy" - 1995
Fugees - "Manifest" - 1996
Outkast - "Babylon" - 1996

CHAPTER 4
Bob Marley - "Redemption Song" - 1980
Ras Tafari Elders - "Kings Highway" - 1991
Sizzla - "Prais Ye Jah" - 1997

CHAPTER 5
Midnite - "Ras to the Bone" - 2000
Capleton - "Jah Jah City" - 2000
Ras Batch - "Sons and Daughters" - 2003

CHAPTER 6
HABESHA Allstars - "HABESHA" - 2003
Warrior King - "Can't Get Me Down" - 2004
Ras Kofi - "Hold On To Your Culture" 2007

CHAPTER 7
Chronixx - "I Can" 2017
Kabaka Pyramid - "Africans Arise" - 2018
Kuami Eugene - "Angela" - 2018

1
INTRODUCTION
DIVINE TIMING

PROVERB: If you think you are too small to make a difference... you haven't spent the night with a mosquito.

(Teena - Cousin) *I'm the youngest of three children born to Harry Myers and Chansey Benjamin. I had a really beautiful childhood, born into a great and very close-knit family located in St. Mary's, Georgia, on my father's side, and Fernandina Beach, Florida, on my mother's side. The foundation of closeness and love has guided me throughout life. It's given me a solid foundation because I've been rooted in that from the beginning. Cashawn, who is technically my second cousin, has always been more like my brother. His grandfather, Raymond Myers, who we call Uncle R.C., and my father are brothers. Uncle R.C. had about seventeen years on my father, so Cashawn's dad and my dad are actually closer in age. My earliest memories of Cashawn and me are us playing together in St. Mary's, Georgia. St. Mary's is a small town, coastal community in Georgia. Country. Everybody knows everyone.*

We have many ancestors. On my father's side, I can go back to my third grandmother, who came from Africa by the name of Bina. That's the only name that we have, Bina. And so Bina had Andrew Myers. Andrew Myers is my great, great-grandfather. Andrew Myers married Mary, and Andrew and Mary had ten children, I believe. I just recently found out that one of those children, Joseph "Joe" Myers, was a twin. So that's really exciting. Joseph married Eva Mae Moody, and they had my grandfather named Ralph Myers. Ralph Myers married Willie Mae Myers.

They had nine children. My father is the ninth child, Harry Myers. Now, on my grandmother Willie Mae's side, her mother's name is Annabel, and her father's name is Alonzo Williams. We have so many parents and grandparents, many of whom I do not know the names of. I am still doing the work to remember them all.

CASHAWN MYERS

(Harry - Uncle) *My name is Harry James Myers. My oldest brother, Ralph James Myers, named me after the trumpet player, Harry James. And I pursued it. I played a clarinet, which is a small version of a trumpet.*

I'm the baby out of nine kids. Cashawn is my grand nephew. His father is my nephew. His grandfather is my brother, Raymond Myers. So Cashawn is my grand nephew, but you know, I just call him nephew. I love the history of our family. When we used to have the Myers family reunion, my brother William would read some of the family history, including the history of our ancestor, Andrew Myers. He was a slave, but when he came to this area from North Carolina, he purchased about 240 acres, what we call Mush Bluff. So that lets you know that even then, my grandparents, great-grandparents, were business-minded, and you can tell that that was passed down to the next generations. We have family members who are carpenters, brick-masons, etc. We know how to build. This home that I'm sitting in right now was built by my nephew. Of course, I did my own wiring, but he built the house. He built the home, and my first cousin did my brickwork for me. So we do things like that. My nephew Russell built about three homes, and I wired them all for him. My nephews Sean and Billy too, so they are all doing something that stems from our grandparents. Now my dad, Mr. Ralph Myers, was something else. He only had a third-grade education, but he was a historian. He could relate back to when he was actually three years of age. When he conversed with somebody, you would think that he had a college education, but that's just how he was. He did a lot of reading. My mother also kept her head in a book. Folks would be amazed by what my father was able to speak about and do with just a third-grade education. He was also a carpenter and an excellent cook.

Most of my family members were also fishermen. My oldest brother actually went missing in 1975 around the Bermuda Triangle, and when they went looking for him, they never saw anything, no debris, no nothing. Our family was industrious; all I can say, really, is that God has always had His hand on us. When I look at my dad now, he's planting, and Raymond, Cashawn's granddad, always had a beautiful garden. I would see him outside, and I would say, "What are you doing out there, Raymond?" He'd be out there talking to his garden. He said, "You have to talk to them." I couldn't do that, you know, (laughs) it was just something new, but, yes, the family had poured a lot into us.

I was one of nine kids. There were five girls and four boys, and my parents were able to send four of us to college. My oldest brother went to the water. He shrimped. My next oldest brother, William, went into the Marine Corps. When he came out, he went to the trade school in Savannah and became a brick mason. My brother Raymond stayed here in St. Mary's and worked with my brother-in-law because he had already established a business. So Raymond and another one of my brothers-in-law worked with Willie Battle. And that's how the family did very well. I attribute it to Jehovah God, actually, having his hands on the family, you know.

I enjoyed my childhood, and I can remember when I first got married and had kids. I remember watching the kids grow up, and Cashawn coming by. He and my son Tyrus would play in the yard for hours, seem like. As Cashawn got older, he would call, and we would just talk. I would try to encourage him because he was doing great things. And I didn't know the extent of it until I started talking with my daughter Teena, but yeah, I'm very proud of him. He has a very good lineage, I would say.

(Rita - Mama) Cashawn comes from a background of educators and farmers, so that's what he does. He educates, and he's into farming and agriculture. When he was younger, he wanted no parts of it, but that's exactly what he does now, so I feel like it's come full circle. He grew up watching both grandfathers. His dad's father always had a garden and planted and did things. My grandfather, my mother's father, always had a garden with grape vines and stuff. And my grandfather would also plow fields for other people's gardens. My father's dad always had gardens. My aunts and I are educators. So Cashawn comes from that background. He had cousins who taught him in school and aunts who were his teachers. So he's just continuing the legacy. He's continuing on and taking it a step *further because now he's on the continent. So he's taking us further, he's still educating and still farming, and he's educating our family about our history, our ancestors, about Ghana and other places he's traveled, about farming.*

He came to my house and helped me plant some things in my planter boxes. He helps us with our eating. He's trying wholeheartedly to get me to be a vegetarian; it's a better and healthier lifestyle for you. So he's honoring us by going back to what we had in the beginning. Going back to what we knew, growing our own food, living a sustainable life, learning to save energy, and not waste. We used to be a people who believed in those things. And I think he's taken us back to some of that through what he's doing. It's allowing us to see what's really important and what we really need and should be doing.

Lyana's Mobile Home in Woodbine, GA

MANNERS WILL TAKE YOU PLACES MONEY WON'T

Granddaddy Kippy and Brama as Teens

Young Mama Rita with Great Grandma Mammie

Cashawn and Mama

Cashawn and Daddy celebrate 1st birthday

2
FOUNDATION
PLANTED IN FERTILE SOIL

PROVERB: If we stand tall, it is because we are standing on the shoulders of those who came before us.

Woodbine, Georgia, is where it all began for me. It's a small rural town in Southeast Georgia on the coast of the Atlantic Ocean, with no more than 3,000 people. It was a small town when I was growing up, and it's probably even smaller now. My Granddaddy Kippy never slept past six. In fact, I'm not sure I've ever even seen him sleep at all. He was the kind of man who was first to wake up and last to lie down. Granddaddy Kippy was a businessman, and he always had some kind of business to attend to. I never saw him work for anyone else in my life. Not only did he work for himself, but he also employed people in the community, making sure others and their families were taken care of. Between him and my other grandfathers - Rose and R.C. - I grew up witnessing self-sufficient men. In St. Mary's, my granddaddy R.C. was a carpenter. He built his own house. My Uncle Harry was an electrician. My Uncle Willie B. had goats, and my Uncle William was a fishing man. Any time I would go to his house, I would be greeted by the smell of firewood as Uncle William brought in his latest catch. These are the types of men that I saw who instilled in me values of work ethic. They ate from the same land they worked.

(**Aunt Geree - *Grand Aunt***) *Cashawn had a big, big family because both the Myers and the Mainor families are large. We were all there for him, and we all did everything that we could. We spoiled him because he was the first one. Cashawn was always everybody's baby. I knew that even if I wasn't there, my brother Kippy was gonna take him up and take him somewhere. He'd just put him in a truck with him and take Cashawn.*

(**Gail - *Little Sister***) *Shawn is my mom's firstborn. She was a teen mom, and I don't say that as a statistic, nor do I say that as a bad thing. She was a teen mom doing the best that she could, and Shawn's a product of* her. My grandparents wanted my mom to still go to college, so she did. My grandma, who we call Brama, and my granddaddy Kippy, were Shawn's caregivers for the first few years of his life while my mom was at school. Then, when she was on holiday and summer break, she had to jump right back into mom mode. So it was like at an early age, Shawn was taught, "Okay, sometimes we sacrifice things for the long run of the family."

My Brama and my granddaddy raised him with love and care, and just the gravitas that he has today. They did this for all of us because my mom went back to school when I was in middle school. She moved back to Camden County, Georgia—the root of our family, the real grass in our soil. She taught high school during the day and went to school at night, and once again, my Brama and Granddaddy stepped in to raise me and my brother Lionel. So their influence shaped all of us.

Our grandparents truly are the backbone of our family. They taught us the importance of family. They taught us the importance of hard work. They taught us the importance of knowing how to cook for yourself. If you don't cook, you don't eat. But not only did they cook, they made everything from scratch and with so much love. And that was passed down to them from their parents and grandparents. That's how they were. They were always there, always very present, no matter what.

"Alright y'all come on out. We ready to sing 'happy birthday.'" Aunt Robin sat next to me as we excitedly watched my mom place the biggest birthday cake I had ever seen down on the table in front of us. Brama, Grandaddy Kippy, Gerard, Tarshia, and my other family came outside as Mama started to light the candles. It was cool this day. Although it was smack dab in the middle of December, being down in south Georgia meant it was still nice enough for us to sit and sing outside. At least on this day.

The cake looked delicious. I didn't have sweets that much growing up, so when we did, it was a special day. "Happy birthday to you. Happy birthday to you," they started to sing. Aunt Robin started dancing next to me. Although she's my aunt, she's only a year or so older than me *because she's the youngest of my grandfather's children. So she always felt more like an older sister than an aunt. Right as the Stevie Wonder rendition was about to end, Aunt Robin scooted closer to the cake, took a deep breath, and blew. I couldn't believe it! She blew out the candles on my cake, on my birthday!*

Growing up in Woodbine, anywhere I went, there seemed to be an aunt, uncle, or god-mom around. I used to walk from school down the main road that goes through all of Woodbine and go straight to Grandma Annie's house. Grandma Annie lived directly across the street from us, and she would watch me until my grandmother, Brama, came home from work. Grandma Annie was a tall, dark skin woman who was stern yet gentle, and man, did she use to feed me *good*! One thing about Grandma Annie, she was a St. Louis Cardinals fan. So we used to watch all the St. Louis Cardinals baseball games. Because of her, I loved Willie McGee and Ozzy Smith, who played for the Cardinals. Interestingly enough, years later, when my mom, siblings, and I moved to Edwardsville, my stepdad, Stump Mitchell, played for the St. Louis Football Cardinals. We used to go to the St. Louis Cardinals baseball games, and I had a chance to meet both Willie McGee and Ozzy Smith. That was special. I used to always think about my Grandma Annie during that time because she really gave me my love for the Cardinals, and I got a chance to see them in person.

Grandma Annie helped take care of me. I didn't learn until later in life that she wasn't even my biological grandmother, but it didn't matter, because she was so important to me growing up.

There were a lot of elderly people on our block, and like Grandma Annie and Miss Beatrice, another one of the elders in the neighborhood who helped look after me, they all pitched in to help take care of me. When I was growing up, from birth to around age six, I lived in a mobile home with my grandmother. My room was on one end, and my grandma's bedroom was all the way on the other side. For the longest time she would try to force me to sleep in the bed by myself. I would always lie down in the bed by myself, and then by the middle of the night, I'd get up and walk down to her room. It's so funny because all my children did, or do, the exact same thing when they were growing up.

I have a lot of fond memories of living with Brama in Woodbine. I remember playing in the yard with Gerard, Jarvis, and Keris, and a lot of my other cousins, just being around people who cared about me, looked out for me, and loved me. Right next to the mobile home was my great-granddaddy Rose's house. I was fortunate enough to be able to spend time with him before he passed. I was about five years old then. At his house, there were fruit trees and a garden area. He used to grow a lot of food, like squash, collard greens, sweet potatoes, and tomatoes. I even remember first drinking coffee with him. I'm grateful I got to know Granddaddy Rose. He left us the house, and after he passed, Brama moved into it. Today, it's our family home, a living piece of the legacy he left behind. The land is his gift to us, and we continue to use and honor it.

(Gerard - Cousin) *On paper, Cashawn is my second cousin, but really, he's a little brother to me. We're only a few months apart, but I was a year ahead of him in school because my birthday is in March and his is in December of the same year. We grew up together - chasing girls, playing in the yard. When we got older, his mom married a pro athlete, and they moved to Atlanta, but whenever he'd come home, our house was the first place he went. He'd come to spend the night. If Shawn and the family came home from Atlanta for a couple of days, a couple of weeks, however long, he'd be here. When they visited over the summer, he'd be here.*

We worked with his grandfather Kippy on his farm, and one of our jobs when we were about eight or nine was shoveling cow manure in his grandfather's field. We would work from about eight to three or four in the afternoon. We did this around four or five days a week, dirty, filthy, all kinds of stuff. His grandfather was a local employer, a businessman. He did a little bit of everything, sold cars, hauled dirt, rented property, whatever, and that too, shaped

Cashawn. We've talked a lot about how his grandfather really taught him about being his own businessman.

***

"Come on Shawn, jump!" Gerard called me from below as I stared down at the water. The water was pitch black, but that was what made it so exciting. It was the middle of the summer and blisteringly hot outside. I couldn't wait to feel the refreshing water on my skin. After a quick countdown from ten, suddenly I was flying in the air, diving into what was surely the coolest water on Earth.

Summers in Woodbine were brutally hot, much like summers in the rest of Georgia and the South in general. So almost every day, or as often as we could, my cousins and I would go to "The Hole." Back in the day, we didn't have a proper swimming pool in Woodbine. So instead, we would find watering holes. That's what we called them, but they were basically these little shallow swamps. There was one not too far from grandaddy Kippy's house that we used to go to. That was the one that all the children loved, but really, most of the children's parents forbade them from going there. The children who went to the hole usually had parents who weren't watching them that closely because all the other parents forbade their children from going.

The hole was a swamp with black water, and nobody there. You could easily drown, but I used to love to go. I only went a few times, though. I used to sneak and go to the hole with my cousins, and that was some of the most fun we had. It was tucked off in the bush, and it's nothing but this super black water, and for hours, you just swim. It was a different kind of freedom.

I had a lot of family around growing up - aunties, uncles, grandparents, but cousins, *they* were abundant. In Woodbine, they have a place we called "The Villas," which is a housing project or an apartment complex. Essentially, it's the hood. I had a few cousins and friends who stayed in the villas, and sometimes I used to spend the night with them. One night I stayed over at my cousins' on a school night. Their parents got up the next morning to get themselves together and went to work, and the expectation was that when it was time for them to wake up, my cousins and I would get ourselves ready and go to school. Well, this morning it was raining, and my cousins decided they didn't want to go to school. There were about five of us there. I was in first grade, and they were all older than me, in the third and fourth grades. So naturally, once they decided they weren't going to go to school, I didn't want to go either. I wanted to hang with them. But my cousins told me, "You got to go to school," so we set off on our walk to Woodbine Elementary, which was about a mile away.

As we're walking from The Villas in the rain, we passed by this grocery store called I.G.A. (Independent Grocers Alliance). I told them I wanted to go inside so I could use the bathroom. As I went inside I.G.A., I devised a plan. I figured that if I hid out in the bathroom long enough, I'd buy some time, and eventually it'd be too late for me to go to school, and they'd let me just stay and hang out with them for the day. Well, so much for that plan, because my cousins came inside and got me out of the bathroom. Then they commenced to walk me to school. Now, mind you, they didn't go to school themselves that day, but they made sure to walk me. In retrospect, I'm grateful that my cousins did that, because it proved that they saw something in me. Although they weren't doing the right thing by skipping school, they didn't want me to go down the same trajectory. So in a way, they protected me from a certain life. Many of those same cousins got into drugs, went to jail, etc., but it was as if they saw something in me that made them say, "You know what, nah, you got a chance to be and do something. We're going to protect you." So, although I was mad then, as I reflected on that incident later in life, I realized that not only telling me I had to go to school, but making sure that I did go by *walking* me, was protection. It was love. They didn't want me to go down the same path, selling drugs and this and that. They wanted me to do something different, to make a life for myself.

Woodbine has always been a place that's protected me. It's been like a shield for me. From just being able to play football out in the yard to everywhere I go, knowing somebody. I truly had relatives all around me. More than anything, I've always felt safe in Woodbine.

The cool thing is though, is that I wasn't only surrounded by elders and young cousins, I was also fortunate enough to have a lot of educated relatives, many of whom ended up being my teachers. I attended the Head Start Program when I was four years old. My Aunt Gloria, Miss Laura, and cousin Diane were not only my relatives but also my teachers. And I just remember how good that was. I actually thought that was how it was supposed to be all the time. Even when I went to Woodbine Elementary, Miss Walker, my kindergarten teacher, was one of my cousins. So a lot of my early teachers were also family members or family friends. And I think that helped me along the way; because my mother had me when she was young, when I went off to school to kindergarten, she was in college at Georgia Southern in Statesboro, so she wasn't around. But I had all of these other women who really were like mothers to me. And again, for me, I thought that was kind of normal. As I grew older, though, I realized how I grew up, particularly living in the rural South, my experience was not necessarily how most people grew up. They don't have this extended family. They don't have extended grandmothers. They don't have all these people who are looking after them. So Woodbine really shaped me, and the people who were a part of my life, especially in the first six to eight years, set the foundation for everything that I do right now. I saw how you're supposed to work together as a community, how you're supposed to raise children.

(**Rita - *Mama***) *As a first-time mom, I knew very little. I babysat my cousins many times because I'm the oldest of the grands, so I knew how to care for a baby, but I had no idea of the long nights I was in for, having to get up in the middle of the night or having to still mother even if I was sick. I was fortunate because my mother was there and she helped me through all of it, but she definitely made sure I was responsible too. She would keep Shawn,* *and then when I got home from school, she would say, "Here's your baby." So there were many nights where I stayed up late, studying with Shawn in my arms.*

It's funny 'cause all of my friends knew him because if I wanted to go to a basketball game, mom would say, "Take your baby." So he was in the yearbook pictures with some of my friends and me at the games. My cousins, friends, and family all helped care for him. Being a first-time mom and a young mom was scary, but my parents made it not so bad because they were there to support me every step of the way. They didn't beat me down for becoming a teenage mother. My father basically said, "Things happen. This is the situation now, and this is how we're going to deal with it. You're going to finish school. We're going to care for the baby." It was never a question of if I'm going to college. It was like, "Okay, you go to college. We're going to keep the baby. We'll work it out." So the support was there from the beginning. Even my granddad, who was still living at the time, helped care for Shawn. I had aunts and uncles whose children Shawn grew up around. They were all there to support. I had a whole village. My grandma Annie was there caring for Shawn; he grew up with her and watched baseball with her because she loved the game. Shawn's dad's parents also helped care for him. We all chipped in, and my family—my village—made it much easier for me because they were there. My mother was there to guide me, and my relatives were there to support me.

✳✳✳

"There's enough you don't know to make another world." Mr. Bryant, one of my teachers at Camden County High School, practically repeated this daily. It had been years since the rainy day my cousins walked me to school while they chose to skip out. Since then, I had worked many days on Granddaddy Kippy's farm, traveled internationally, became an older brother, and learned a little bit more about how the world works.

I never saw my parents together as a couple. By the time I was born, they had gone their separate ways. During the first few years of my life, my mom finished high school and went on to college while I was raised by the village - my grandparents, aunts and uncles, and grew up around a lot of cousins. Although my dad wasn't there in Woodbine, he played a vital role in my childhood development.

I was five the first time I got on a plane. I flew from Jacksonville to Dallas-Fort Worth. My dad, who was in the Army, was stationed in Fort Worth, Texas, and I was visiting for the summer. Coming from Woodbine, being surrounded by family from the moment I was born, made this trip a pretty big deal. I mean, not only was I barely able to read or write, but I was flying on a plane by myself, completely alone. I remember being in the front part of the plane. It was me and this little white boy who also looked to be about five years old. Back then, if you were really young, traveling on a plane like we were, they had a stewardess monitor you to make sure you were taken care of. So there we were, two little five-year-olds traveling from Florida to Texas, and this boy tells me that he wants to tell me a joke. He started off the joke with "Polly wanna cracker, Polly wanna cracker." Then he told me to repeat it to him, "Polly wanna cracker, Polly wanna Cracker." And then when I repeated, "Polly wanna Cracker, Polly wanna Cracker," he said, "Nigger wanna watermelon," and started laughing.

Even though at that time, I didn't understand what he was saying, maybe I had heard the word before, I'm not sure, but I knew how I felt, and that I didn't feel good about the joke. The "joke" wasn't even funny to me. And I just sat there wondering, *what's funny about that joke?* It wasn't until later in life that I realized that he didn't even really know what he was saying. He had been taught something from the people around him, either his parents or others, and simply repeated what he was taught to think was funny. This was my first experience of racism that I remember, and it ingrained in me the feeling of being different because of who I am. This would stick with me for life.

The value of traveling was instilled in me at a young age, seeing other parts of the world and being exposed to other people, having experiences that were great, and some moments that were not so great. I never even went to the same school for more than two years in a row until I got to college.

After spending the first five years of my life with my family in Woodbine, I went to first grade in Plant City, Florida, which is in the Tampa area, with my mom, where she was a high school teacher. After a year, I came back to Woodbine and went to school at Woodbine Elementary. I traveled internationally for the first time when I was eight years old and heading to the third grade. I flew by myself all the way to Hanau, Germany, to live with my dad for a year. Back then, that was a 12 or 13-hour flight.

Moving to Germany was a tough experience for me. I spent a good deal of my time being homesick and missing my normal comforts and family. Probably the only thing that made it a little better was when my aunt Yvette and my cousin Jason came a few months after I got out there. At least now I was around someone who I knew from the United States. Jason was much younger than me, but it made all the difference to have family around in such a new environment.

For fourth grade, I came back to the U.S. and went to school in Kingsland. Kingsland is in the same county as Woodbine, but it's a different city. That's where I spent a lot of time over at Aunt Verdell's and my cousin Tarshia's house. By fifth grade, I found myself moving again, but this time, with my mom and my stepdad. My mom had gotten married, and I now had a stepdad who was a professional football player in St. Louis, Missouri. He played for the St. Louis Cardinals, so we moved to the outskirts of St. Louis, in Edwardsville, Illinois. I was there for fifth and sixth grade, and during that time, I had graduated to big brother status. My little sister Gail and little brother Lionel were born.

Then I moved back to Georgia to live with my father in Lithonia in seventh and eighth grade. He had come back from the military and moved to the Metro Atlanta area. In 9th grade, I lived in Arizona with my mom and siblings, and in 10th grade, we moved to Stone Mountain, Georgia. In 11th grade, I moved back to Kingsland, where I had lived in fourth grade, and in 12th grade, I was back in Stone Mountain to complete high school at Redan High.

(**John Johnson - Friend**) *I think Cashawn and I met at basketball tryouts in high school. My first impression of him was that he was a cool guy. I was trying out for the junior varsity team, and he was encouraging me to try out for the varsity team. I didn't have confidence that I could play at a varsity level, but Cashawn kept trying to encourage me. I ended up trying out for the JV team and making it. I think that was the 10th grade.*

From what I remember in high school, we just were having fun getting to know people, going around the different schools, and really starting to build our friendship, just creating a bond. We were just young teenagers having fun. When Shawn got his first car, a Volkswagen Beetle, he had it painted. Then he had these wheels put on it, and it looked really good, and when we drove to school for the first time, I can clearly remember the reaction that he got from people. They were loving it, so that was a fun moment. We also did a lot of silly stuff, like driving through the drive-through backwards, just to see what they would say when we got to the window.

We were into music too. Cashawn actually introduced me to the Wu-Tang Clan. Cashawn lived down in the cul-de-sac on my street, and he came up to my house one day when I was building a speaker box for a car stereo system. He helped me build it. So we had some good times. We had a lot of mutual friends too, who we would hang out with, go to parties with, have little get-togethers, and stuff like that. We explored a lot. Shawn and I used to ride around and go downtown, and we even went to Freaknik one year. His cousin had a lowrider truck, and he drove up from Woodbine and let us use it to hang out at Freaknik. We got stuck in traffic and ended up having to stay down there overnight, sleeping in the truck because we couldn't get out. But it was a really fun time—exploring, being out there, and being part of something that later became history. Those are some of my fond memories from our high school days.

Cashawn was very likable, an athlete who played basketball and was fairly popular among our crowd. Not a troublemaker, he just liked to have fun, experience high school and teenage life, chase after girls here and there, and enjoy life. From what I remember, he was also a good student. Since we lived on the same street, we spent a lot of time together, and I got to know his mother, his siblings, and some of his extended family. It was almost like going to school with a cousin or a family member—tight-knit, dealing with whatever comes with being in school, and just enjoying being friends. We were loyal friends, having fun, being high schoolers, and yes, jocks.

Towards the end of our high school years, he started showing interest in some of the things he's still doing today. Even though it's been about 30 years. Looking back, I realize he's always been ambitious and driven. When he went away to college, we went our separate ways—I went to Alabama—but when we reconnected during summers at home, he would teach me about his religion and the things he was passionate about at the time. It reminded me of how focused he's always been, always working toward his goals. Ever since the day I met him, he's been driven to achieve, and I'm proud to see how far he's come.

MANNERS WILL TAKE YOU PLACES MONEY WON'T

Young Cashawn
(5 or 6 years old)

Young Cashawn
the Business Man
(5-6 yrs)

Cashawn (far right) at Redan Elementary

Cool Cashawn,
11th grade, 1993

Cashawn (10th grade) and family -
Mama Rita, Gail, and Lionel

Tarshia, Cashawn, & Brama

3
TRANSFORMATION
COLLEGE & CULTURAL IDENTITY

PROVERB: Once you make up your mind to cross a river by walking through, you do not complain of getting your stomach wet.

After high school, I was off to college in Tallahassee, Florida at Florida Agricultural and Mechanical University (FAMU). I spent all four years of college there.

(**Dr. Jackson-Lowman - *Professor***) *One of the courses that I taught when I came to FAMU in 1996 was Psychology of Black Women. Cashawn was in my class, and out of all the classes I taught, that was probably one of the most dynamic ones. I still have a very vivid memory of that particular class. In that class, I put the students in all kinds of groups. They each had to do a project that was somehow related to Black women. Cashawn was in the group that worked on rights and passage. They did an excellent job on that assignment.*

Cashawn was always a very focused student. Not only bright, because we have a lot of bright students, but truly focused. He just seemed to have a clear sense of his direction and what it is he wanted to do with his life. And that was very interesting because he chose to be in this particular group around rights and passage, and to now see how that area of focus and interest continued to evolve and manifest in his life is amazing. Cashawn was a very committed and devoted student. I could tell that he was very centered, and frankly, probably quite mature for his age, despite the fact that he wasn't older than any of the other students.

During my time at FAMU, I spent a lot of time in Lee Hall, which was this building that had a big auditorium where all the lecturers came. We had all kinds of speakers come through there, who spoke on various topics. But there are two speakers, in particular, who were really instrumental in my growth, whom I had a chance to meet in person.

One was Dr. John Henrik Clarke, whom I met in 1997 before he passed away. Meeting him was such a powerful, powerful experience. He actually has a saying that I still use today, "Service is the greatest form of prayer." When I heard that at the time as a 21-year-old or 22-year-old, it changed my whole way of looking at faith, spirituality, etc.

Another person that I had a chance to meet was Ayi Kwei Armah. Many may know him from 2000 Seasons and some of his other books. He's a Ghanaian writer who writes fiction, but his storytelling is so close to nonfiction—in the way he details the narrative and connects it to the plight of African people on the continent—that it reads almost like a true account. I had the chance to meet Ayi Kwei Armah and even acted as his assistant for the day during his lecture at FAMU. I got to hear his thoughts on a wide range of topics—from Kwame Nkrumah, whom he knew personally, to the state of Black people in America. It was an experience I will never forget.

It was powerful for me to meet those two Pan-African pillars while a student at FAMU. I had the chance to sit at the feet of elders who are truly legends. That was also the first time, in the same Lee Hall, that I got to see Nyahbinghi elders. During a Black History Month event, Nyahbinghi elders traveled from New York and Washington, D.C., and that event gave me my first peep into Rastafari—without me even knowing what I was getting into.

Growing up, most of the positive expressions of the Black experience in America that I saw were centered around sports. I loved seeing Black quarterbacks because that position is always seen as the one requiring the most intelligence and leadership. For the longest time, there was a stereotype that Black people couldn't play quarterback because they didn't have the mental capacity, so Black players were often kept out of that role. Seeing quarterbacks like Warren Moon, Randall Cunningham, and Doug Williams was huge for me—they were early Black quarterbacks I looked up to. That became a way for me to connect with my Blackness, to see myself reflected in those moments of excellence.

And more broadly, I just loved seeing Black people winning—whether in football, basketball, or other sports—like Magic Johnson versus Larry Bird. That's how I expressed my Blackness when I was younger.

It wasn't until I got to FAMU that I began to experience and express my Blackness in a more well-rounded and mature way. And it wasn't just because of my environment and the Black excellence I saw every day on campus; it also had a lot to do with the music I was listening to. This was around the time that the group Outkast came out; it was around '94 with the release of their debut album Southernplayalisticadillacmuzik. That album was monumental for my growth and development because it reflected parts of me—the cool, laid-back side, but also this curiosity I had about something deeper, something missing. Around that time, I began asking bigger questions, trying to understand what was really going on. Outkast presented those ideas in a way I could connect with, and their music helped guide me further along my journey of self-discovery.

If you think about Outkast—from Southernplayalisticadillacmuzik to ATLiens—you can see how the evolution of their music reflected their growth in consciousness. In some ways, I saw my own consciousness grow alongside theirs. I remember the day ATLiens came out: I was at FAMU and went straight to the record store as soon as it opened. I grabbed the album, went back to my dorm, put it on the record player, and experienced banger after banger. Compared to Southernplayalisticadillacmuzik, this album had a more mature vibe—they had taken it to the next level. And I felt myself elevating to that next level in my own growth. It was also around the time I connected with the Black psychology department. Outkast was helping me scratch the surface, and then, once I hit my stride with Black psychology, it felt like everything just came together—they were overloading me with insight, inspiration, and perspective.

And it wasn't just Outkast who made an impression on me; Goodie Mob did too. Outkast came out in '94, and Goodie Mob followed in '95.

That year, Goodie Mob actually headlined FAMU's Homecoming show. Both groups played a big role in shaping my musical consciousness. A few years later, The Fugees dropped The Score, and that took everything to the next level!

I would go from listening to music in my dorm straight to lectures at Lee Hall. Along the way, friends like James, Dedan, and Jerome were part of that journey too. We were constantly building and learning together. I started reading books like Behold a Pale Horse and following speakers like Steve Cokely, who was a regular in Tallahassee at the Aakhet Center run by Drs. Sharan and Dana Denard. That center was the hub for the Black consciousness circuit at FAMU. Anyone and everyone came through. You'd see Steve Cokely, Dr. Afrika, and others, all passing through the same network. At the same time, I had the chance to engage with incredible elders and scholars, like Dr. Clark and Ayi Kwei Armah. I helped Dr. Kobi Kambon when he needed it, getting the chance to sit at the feet of true legends.

All of these experiences elevated my consciousness. The readings reinforced it—books like Ivan Van Sertima's Black Women of Antiquity and his African Origins series, covering Early Asia, Early Europe, and the Americas, provided the foundation. Those books and experiences set the stage for everything that followed.

I took an Intro to Psychology course during my sophomore year. My professor, Dr. Robinson, showed us a snippet of an episode of a film series called "Free Your Mind." The series featured a man named Dr. Asa Hilliard, whom I had never heard of. He was talking about this place called "Kemet." He spoke about Ancient Kemet and what the word "Kemet" means, and who the originators of the Pyramids were. He spoke about where Pythagoras stole his knowledge from and how he went back to Greece and proclaimed himself to be the founder of what we now know as the Pythagorean Theorem. I was so intrigued because I had never heard any of this before. Before college, most of what I knew about Black history or Black excellence came through sports.

I didn't know much about true Black history. I had learned about Dr. King and Harriet Tubman, but that was about it. So when Dr. Hilliard started talking about ancient Kemet and the Kemites, broke down the real history behind the Pythagorean theorem, and explained how so much of what we're taught about Europe and European "intellectuals" was actually taken from African consciousness and African schools of thought—and then recycled as their own—it completely flipped everything I thought I understood.

After class, I asked the professor if I could borrow the VHS tape so that I could watch the full episode. She agreed, and I subsequently went home, watched that tape probably about three or four times before the next class, and within the next few days, the trajectory of my life had completely changed. I went from not being interested in reading, not being interested in really learning, to gobbling up books, learning more within the next semester than I had in the first 21 years of my life.

I changed my major from Physical Therapy to Psychology and immersed myself in the Psychology department, which at that time was the only African-centered psychology department in the country. That became the foundation of where I began to build my knowledge and where I began to put myself on the trajectory that I'm currently on. But it wasn't just because of the knowledge I was gaining.

(**Dedan - Friend**) *The first time I met Cashawn was at Redan High School, right after I had transferred from Southwest DeKalb High School in Decatur, Georgia. My family had moved over to Hidden Hills. I fell in with the guys over there in Stone Mountain; we all hooped back then. So I started playing. One day, we went up to the school to shoot some hoops. There was actually a church next to the gym, and that was where we ended up playing over the summer. This was going into my 11th-grade year. Everyone was in the gym hooping when I noticed this tall, slender guy who could really dribble. I thought, "Oh man, here's some real competition." That was my first time meeting Cashawn. We played ball that day, and from there, we clicked. The rest, as they say, is history.*

We had a lot of fun back in the day. We lived, hung out, went to football games, partied—Cashawn was no different. He loved to turn up and hype up the party, and those were some good times. I remember that after he left Redan, he went down south to finish school, and then after we graduated, he went to FAMU while I went to Morehouse. During one winter or summer break, he came back wearing a dashiki. At the time, my consciousness was still new, and I probably made a joke about it, caught up in some of my old, ignorant mentalities. But as I listened to him share information and saw how true he was to expanding his awareness, I realized he was making a profound change. He was one of the first people in my peer group who really expanded his consciousness toward African awareness and the African liberation movement.

Some people jokingly say I'm double-cursed, and while I know they mean it lightly, I also understand where they're coming from. I don't believe I'm cursed, per se, but on both sides of my family—the Myers and the Mainors—the men were known for having multiple women, multiple wives, and living that kind of lifestyle became the expectation. Growing up, people would tell me, "Oh yeah, I know you gonna have plenty girls after you." In their minds, that was a compliment, and I internalized it. In high school, a lot of the music I listened to portrayed women as sex objects. The artists weren't elevating women; they were calling them out their name, and as a teenager, that's what we saw as normal. So between my family lineage and the music, it can be traced back even further to practices during enslavement when the Black family structure was destroyed. Women were often not around to raise their own children because they were caring for white children or were separated from their families entirely. Even in African contexts, where multiple wives existed, it was part of a structured family system—not chaos. What we inherited in America, however, was a broken family system. That environment, combined with the music, shaped the mindset I grew up with. Choosing to rise above it now felt like swimming upstream. Respecting women was not the norm I saw in everyday life. At FAMU and later in Atlanta, where the ratio was ten or fifteen to one women to men, men were expected to juggle multiple relationships. That mindset followed me through high school—my nickname was even "Pimp C," and I was known for dating multiple women at once.

Over time, I had to grow and elevate from that way of moving and being. Between the knowledge I was gaining, the conscious music I was listening to, the lectures I attended, and the pillars I was meeting, a shift began to occur. Truthfully, around this time, I was looking for a challenge. I wanted to challenge myself in a way I had never been challenged before. On the ATLiens album, Andre 3000 had a verse on the song "Growing Old" that really stood out to me: "I bet you never heard of a playa with no game, told the truth to get what I want, but shot it with no shame." That line inspired me to challenge myself. I was used to having multiple girlfriends or female friends, and I would communicate with them as if they were the only one. So I wanted to challenge myself to be straight up with them and let them know the truth, what was really going on. So I started with one. I had been seeing this girl at FAMU for a few weeks. We enjoyed each other's company, but like my other "relationships," it was nothing too serious. One day, we were hanging out at the dorms, and I told her simply, "You are not the only one," and that I did not want to pursue anything other than a friendship. I wasn't sure what to expect in telling her the truth, maybe sadness, maybe anger, I just knew that I had to tell her the truth. Not only did I owe it to her, but I owed it to the version of me that I was becoming.

As a result of confiding in her, she encouraged me to tell the others that I was dating. She said everyone needed to know. And so that's what I set out to do. But sometimes when you do wrong, life has a way of correcting your wrongs before you finally get around to doing it.

Initially, everything was cool. I didn't have any specific plans around when to tell each girl, but I had every intention to do so. Back in the day, they had something called Star 69. When you dialed that on a landline phone, it allowed you to view the phone number of the last caller and automatically call that number if you wanted to. Well, one day I was over at my "main" girlfriend's house, and I called another girlfriend because I was headed to see her next. You can probably guess what happened. After I left the main girl's house, the other girlfriend dialed *69, and my main girlfriend's mother answered. Not only did they talk to each other, but their mothers also spoke to each other. Needless to say, it was a mess. I ended up being found out before I had a chance to tell everyone.

This was a pivotal moment in my life because it created a whole bunch of chaos, uncertainty, but more than anything, pain. That experience was the first time that I saw pain in someone that I cared about, and that impacted me deeply. I wanted each girl to feel special, like she was the only one, and not necessarily because I was trying to get over on them, but because I really did care. But when I saw how finding out the truth, especially the way they did, hurt them, it pained me. I knew then that I couldn't be that way again. I had to transform myself.

That entire experience was part of what pushed me to transform how I interacted with women. It was then that I decided to take time to focus on myself, to really understand who I am and what I stand for. The first girl I was honest with became my first female friend. She helped me see that women weren't just there to be pursued. Although our friendship lasted only until the end of the school year, it gave me a new perspective. After taking that time for self-reflection, I decided that when I re-engaged with women, I would do so with full transparency.

For roughly three months, I cut off all interaction with women I had been involved with and closed myself off to any new relationships. During that time, I focused entirely on myself. As I evaluated and reshaped my relationship with women, I continued to study and learn, and these two experiences went hand in hand. My rise in consciousness and my growth in how I related to women happened simultaneously—the higher my awareness became, the more mature and grounded my relationships grew.

Taking time for myself was a major impetus for my growth and development. I began to realize that I had been perpetuating some of the dysfunction from my own family lineage, especially in how I interacted with women. I started to see how some of my actions negatively affected the women in my life and others I cared about, yet I hadn't taken the time to consider their feelings or the impact of my behavior. This period of self-reflection coincided with my first psychology course. My mind was absorbing information about Africa and Black history while I simultaneously went through an inner purge, examining how I operated—particularly in my relationships with women. Reflecting on my interactions with Black women opened me up to understanding who I truly am. The more I came to know myself, the more I could uplift and honor Black women through my words and actions. For me, these two journeys—self-discovery and rise in consciousness as an African man—were inseparable. My perspective on women was completely shaped by my growing awareness of my own identity.

During this time, I was doing a lot of reading and reflecting. I prayed and asked the Most High that, when the time came to re-engage with women, I would be completely transparent—sharing my past experiences and how I had treated women before. I wanted anyone who met me to know exactly who I am and who I've been. Doing that freed me and opened me up to receive at the right moment—and that's when I met Shevon.

CASHAWN MYERS

LOVE LETTER TO THE BLACK WOMAN

Dear Black woman, mother of humanity, first to walk the earth, creator of all humankind.
We thank you for the work that you have done for us.
Dear Black woman, we thank you for being our first teacher,
For being the first to give us unconditional love,
For being the first to show humanity to the world.
Even though in these modern times you don't get the respect, the love, and the consideration that you deserve,
I, as a Black man, want you to know that you are loved and you are respected,
And it is well deserved. You have been the first to make sure that our generations continue, always sacrificing and putting yourself above others.

There's an African proverb that says, "When a mother is hungry, the first question she asks is, 'What can I get to feed the children?'"
That's always been the example of the Black woman, always considering the family and I want to let you know that, Black woman, you are appreciated.
For our Black girls, stand firm in who you are.
Stay rambunctious. Stay sassy, as they call it. That's really your confidence.
Know who you are. Be comfortable in your Black skin. Be comfortable in your natural hair. Be comfortable in your natural body and know that no other standard of beauty can fit your perfection.
For all of my sisters, know that we, as Black men, we love you.
We would never be where we are without you. We need you to continue on.
Don't be discouraged. Don't be frustrated. Know that we are not against each other, and we are actually the perfect match.
There's nothing that the Black man and Black woman together can't accomplish.

So let's stay strong, let's stay connected so that we can build the Black family.
We need you, Black woman. We need you to continue to be strong, holding in your divine feminine, yet also being able to lead at all times when needed.
You are the perfect example of what it means to be the best all around. The most beautiful, the most intelligent, the most loving, and the most fierce if you cross her.
We want you to continue to be YOU, Black woman. Don't change for anyone.
Continue to uplift yourself, uplift others, and uplift the Black family because without that, we wouldn't be where we are.

There are so many examples of powerful Black women throughout our story that we can't name them all,
but we know that all of the ones that have been there to uplift their people, we remember you, we remember your spirit.
So we ask you, Black woman, to continue to shine your light. Don't dim it for anyone.
Even when society tells you that you're not beautiful enough, when they tell you you're not good enough,
We know that you are the standard bearer, so we tell you, Black woman, that we will continue to uplift you.
We will continue to shower you with blessings and we will continue to acknowledge the contribution that you've made on the world and in our story.
So Black woman, we love you. Black woman, we uplift you. Black woman, continue to be the shining example that you are.

With Love,

Cashavn Myus

Cashawn at FAMU

Cashawn with Grandaddy Kippy on the Farm in Woodbine

4
CULTIVATION
COMMUNITY WORK & FAMILY LEGACY

PROVERB: *Dreaming of eating won't satisfy the hungry man.*

I can say that my life changed when I was at FAMU, but it was not just because my awareness of myself and the strength and power of my people grew; it was also because of the woman in my life.

I met Shevon, my wife of 26 years, in 1996. I was a sophomore at FAMU and she was living in Stone Mountain, going to Dekalb College. It was summer break, so we both happened to be in Atlanta, where we were living at the time.

(Shevon - Wife) *Cashawn and I met when he called into my job. I was working in the photo lab in Eckerd's, which later became Rite Aid, and is now CVS. Cashawn called with very specific details about one of the photos that he had. He wanted it to fit a certain way in this frame. So, me being a kind-hearted person, providing good customer service is important, it's what we're supposed to do. So I'm tending to him on the phone, and he's telling me what time he gets off work and asking me to please not close the lab because he really needed to get this done before going back to school. And so I was like, "Okay, as long as you get here before the lab closes, I'll try my best to help you." And so, you know, he being himself, he was very flirtatious on the phone, asking me not to close the lab, and I was like, well, you better get here on time if you want that picture done. Anyway, he got there right before we closed, and so I started working with him on the picture. So then I guess him being the person that he is, he came behind the counter. Being that we're about to close, my manager is no longer there. So Shawn came behind the counter because he was very specific about how he wanted this picture. And so we're cutting, slicing, dicing, doing all this, trying to get this picture exactly like he wants it. I think he had a picture he shot vertically, and he wanted it to fit horizontally, something to that effect. He was playing pool, and it was a great shot of him, you know,* *he looked very focused on shooting the pool. So we're printing out, cutting, pasting, and doing all these different things, just trying to get it right. Next thing you know, the store was getting ready to close. I believe the lab closed around six, while the store closed around nine. So we're back there working on this picture, and every minute something comes out, he doesn't like it. So we have to go back to the drawing board, trying to get it right. But throughout the time that we were working on the picture, we were talking, and the way we interacted with each other was as if we had known each other forever. I learned that he went to Redan High School, and I went to Redan. I don't even remember some of what we talked about, but we were just talking and working, talking and working. Then finally, when I thought we had it down right, we're sending it through the printer again when he tells me, "I'm gonna go to Dairy Queen, do you want a banana split?" And I was like, "Sure." You know, I was back there putting in the work, so I was like, "yeah." So then he went out the door and came back shortly thereafter because the Dairy Queen, which was right across the street, was closed. In fact, most of the things in the area were closed because it was already nine o'clock. So I'm just like, "Okay, cool." I guess my energy and the way I am is just, whatever I can do to help you, I will try my best. So I was not really giving it much thought. He was handsome, and we were just vibing, really. And then as we were leaving the store, 'cause now the store is guaranteed to close, his picture came out. He still wasn't all the way sold on the picture because you could still see some hint of where we connected it, and him being the perfectionist that he is, he wasn't entirely satisfied. But at this point, I'm thinking that we've been at this all evening, and now I'm ready to go. So then he asks me, "You wanna go to the movies?" And at that point, I had forgotten that it was actually a weeknight, not even a weekend, but I said, "Yeah, why not?" So then he checked all the movies that were playing, and because it was a weekday, we had just missed all the latest movie starting times. So the movies wasn't going to happen. So then he was like, "Well, you want to go for a ride?" So I was like, "Listen, I have to get home and get dressed." So I went to my friend's house, who wasn't that far from where I worked, and got ready over there.*

Now, at that time, we didn't have cell phones; all we had were pagers. So I told my friend that I'll be with this guy, and if you don't hear from me by a certain time, page me. I told her who he was and she knew him because she also had gone to Redan.

So Cashawn was driving, but he was going in a direction I wasn't familiar with. I asked him where we were going, and we ended up at Piedmont Park. We sat there, and Cashawn talked the entire time, like three hours plus. He talked, and I just sat there and listened. I didn't say much. He spoke about everything, just in terms of dating and his shortcomings and mistakes that he had made when he had dated. He just went through this whole dialogue, and so I'm sitting there like, "Hmm, do I continue seeing him? Because he has a lot going on, just in terms of dating two people at the same time and feeling very distraught because he had hurt both of them." So I'm just like, wow, you know, but no judgment. Like I said, I just listened.

Then after he dropped me off at my friend's, I'm thinking, "He's, he's a lot," but I think that's what led us to each other, the fact that I didn't judge. I was like, "Okay, I'm not sure what they had going on, but I'm my own person. This is me, this is how I show up in my relationship." He also vowed that night that the next person he met, which ended up being me, he would have like this whole rebirth of how he would show up in that relationship. And honestly, the rest has been history.

The first night I met her, I was at Eckerds, looking to get some photos developed. She happened to be there, and she assisted me through this process of getting these photos. There was definitely chemistry. I invited her to have some ice cream at Dairy Queen across the street afterwards. Well, Dairy Queen was closed. So then I said, "Well, look, let's kick it for a little while." So I invited her to come to Piedmont Park. It was probably like 10, 11 o'clock at night at this point, but she agreed to come. We had just met. We went to Piedmont Park, and at Piedmont Park, from the time we were there, probably like 12 a.m. to 3 a.m., I told her my life story. All of the women, everything. So she had this baseline. After that, I went home that night, got up the next morning, and when I saw my dad, he asked me how everything was. I told him I met someone and I said I'm gonna marry her that night. Why? Because after I told her everything, I asked her if she still wanted to deal with me, and she was like, "Yeah."

Although we both graduated from Redan High School, I was a year ahead of her, our paths never crossed back then. In hindsight, that was probably for the best. I wasn't in the mindset to take women seriously at that point, and I likely would've repeated the same patterns I had with others. Nothing happens before its time.

(**Shevon - Wife**) *Our meeting was all Divine. We literally met at my job; he was coming from work, and I was in my lab coat. There was no getting all dolled up and putting on a certain image. It was just us, real and raw, in our element, working together. And that's what we've been doing ever since.*

When I first met Cashawn, I felt like he was spontaneous. He also had things going for himself. And of course, he was handsome. Let's not forget or act like the physical doesn't matter because it definitely does. So I was willing to see how things would turn out. I actually was talking to someone at the time, though, but I think what stood out about Cashawn was his spontaneity. He also planned things. He was at FAMU, and he would come to Atlanta every other weekend. And every time he came he had something different planned, and I'm like, "Oh, I like this." It's not like having someone relying on you to plan everything. You know, it was quite different. And so he won my heart from the other person because the other person was just waiting for me to do everything. Cashawn and I also traveled because he worked at Delta Airlines over the summer. So we went to St. Croix, we went here, we went there, just traveling all over; and so I think all those things were very impressionable on me.

Shevon became a huge part of my life in a powerful way. As we dated, we continued our studies at our respective universities - me at FAMU and her at Dekalb College, and then Albany State University, but our lives quickly intertwined. We learned about and with each other. We shared a love for our people and our culture, and we shared a love for travel. One of our first trips together was actually to Shevon's home country, Guyana. We went during the winter break of 1997. We spent two weeks there, and I got to meet a lot of her family. We stayed with her aunt and uncle. When we came back, we started a coconut oil-based hair brand called "Kube Oil." The word "kube" means "coconut" in the Akan language of Ghana. I did not know then how the naming of this oil would foreshadow our connection to Ghana later in life.

***

After I graduated from FAMU, I moved to Washington, D.C. to attend Howard University to attain my Master's Degree. I had earned my Bachelor's in Psychology and had set my sights on Howard because I was ready to explore the world around me. D.C., being considered the "Mecca" for Black people at the time, seemed like the right place to go. It was 1998, and Shevon and I's relationship was progressing. We continued to date while I was now a graduate student at Howard, and she then became a student at Georgia State University. After spending a year in D.C. by myself, Shevon left Atlanta and joined me in the fall of 1999 when we found out that she was pregnant. We married that year, and on January 15, 2000, we welcomed our first of six children into the world, Kidane Negus Myers. That was a transformative experience because now, not only did I have to live for myself, not only did I have to live for Shevon, but I had a whole other life that I helped to bring forth that I had to live for. So it gave me a whole next level of focus, a next level of seriousness, and became my protection.

My time in D.C. was life-changing. I had begun to build community in Washington, D.C., particularly with the Ras Tafari community. Since I was a graduate student, I moved around on and off Howard's campus often. It was at Howard where my mind really expanded beyond the national borders of America. I met so many people of African descent from all over the world and truly saw our connection as African people from a holistic perspective. It was in D.C. where my connection to the Ras Tafari faith became rooted for life.

My journey to Ras Tafari really began through knowledge of self. It goes back to my time as a student at FAMU—getting that video of Dr. Hilliard, studying ancient civilizations, reading John G. Jackson's Introduction to African Civilization, Cheikh Anta Diop, and many of the greats who wrote about ancient Ethiopia as the true cradle of humankind. Coupled with that was my early experience growing up and attending church with Grandma Annie, Brama, and other family members. My grandmother and other family members would take us to different churches. I wasn't really "in" the church like that—you go to Sunday school, see your friends, your cousins, have fun, then go to vacation Bible camp in the summer. But it was always with this European-looking Jesus, and I never fully connected to it. I just went because that's what you were expected to do. Spiritually, though, I always knew there was a higher being, a Creator. I had never really put much thought into my connection to a higher power—how I connected, why I connected, or where those beliefs even came from. So, as I started learning about ancient Ethiopia and African history in general, that study led me on a journey. It began with learning about ancient Kemet, then understanding Ethiopia as the mother of Kemet, and eventually, all of that came full circle for me through music. I would say the first real spark or recognition of that came through the Fugees—their music, their references, and even the mention of Haile Selassie on The Score album. Their work, along with how they incorporated Bob Marley into their sound (even Wyclef's version of "No Woman, No Cry"), kept leading me forward. From the Fugees, I started listening more deeply to Bob Marley, his praises to Emperor Haile Selassie I, and the biblical passages and speeches of His Majesty that he quoted. All of that pushed me to start questioning, to ask more, and to figure out exactly where these pieces fit into my own understanding.

It was around this time that things deepened even more. A brother, whom I ended up being roommates with, Tarik, taught me a little bit more about His Imperial Majesty, Emperor Haile Selassie I, through the Nyabinghi Order. Then one day, he told me he was going to a gathering. He said he was going to a Binghi and asked me if I wanted to go. I said, yeah, of course. When we arrived, it was a three-story house in D.C. on 10th Street, and there were these Rastafari elders. Everybody was seated, and they were in a meeting talking about the order of the day, different activities, and things that they were planning. Then they closed out the meeting with this powerful drumming.

This drumming had a very slow rhythmic pace to it, similar to a heartbeat, and with that drumming came this chanting of these words, they continued to say over and over and over and over again. This went on for about 20 or so minutes, and just in that small amount of time that I was there, something resonated with me, from the drums, the chants, the reasoning.

That experience led me on a journey to do more research. I began to research ancient biblical history because they were also quoting biblical passages, one being in Genesis chapter two, talking about the land where Mount Zion is, where heaven or earth is. So when I read it for myself and saw Ethiopia represented in the Bible, it gave me a whole new perspective—first on the Bible, and second on everything I'd been learning about this ancient land from the history books I'd been reading, like George Jackson and others. Now it all tied together: what Ras Tafari saw, how Ras Tafari connected to this ancient land, and what I was coming to understand for myself.

That initial research then led me on a deeper journey to really connect more with Ethiopia and to learn more about His Imperial Majesty Emperor Haile Selassie I. I ended up connecting with an elder brother who was a part of the Ras Tafari community. He shared with me that His Imperial Majesty had actually come to Howard University, received an honorary degree of law from Howard University in 1954, and left artifacts and gifts to the University. Learning this information ignited me even more. To know that I was now a student at Howard University—a place His Imperial Majesty himself had visited—made everything hit differently. I was learning about him, reading about him, seeing how deeply he was connected to African unity and this ancient kingdom that stretches back thousands of years, and it all really began to intrigue me. That, along with attending more Rastafari gatherings—especially the Nyahbinghi gatherings on Saturdays—and having more reasonings with the elders, just solidified for me who Rastafari is and who Haile Selassie is. And it all tied in so closely with where I was in my own life: living plant-based and vegan, using the holy herbs, being environmentally sustainable, and being Pan-African to the core.

All of these principles were exactly where I was transforming at that time, as I was gaining this knowledge of self. And Rastafari became the vehicle and mechanism that grounded it for me. In particular, seeing His Majesty—how he had attained such a respected status, recognized by universities, focused on building Africa and helping unite the continent—just made sense. Then, tying that in with the anciency of the Solomonic dynasty, knowing His Majesty comes from the lineage of King David, King Solomon, and the Queen of Sheba, all these names I had heard throughout my life, whether through the Bible or textbooks, it suddenly clicked that he was the culmination of that history. And then, of course, there was the prophecy in Revelation about all making war against the Lion and the Lion defeating them—the Conquering Lion of the Tribe of Judah. Learning how His Imperial Majesty defeated the Italians before World War II, and seeing that moment as part of that prophecy, brought everything into alignment for me. It reaffirmed Haile Selassie as the returning ancestral realm of the creative force we know as the Most High in flesh, manifesting in so many ways. It was perfect alignment.

I continued to read. I read His Majesty's autobiography, *My Life in Ethiopia's Progress*, Parts 1 and 2, and speeches of His Majesty, and everything aligned to Haile Selassie being the one who was chosen to sit on that throne and have life eternal. That understanding has influenced everything that I've done from my time as a student at Howard University up until now. It influences how I move and the things that I put my energy into, from being a family man to knowing that I'm a community leader, a nation builder, a diplomat. His Majesty also received an honorary Doctorate of Agriculture and over fifteen honorary Doctorate of Law degrees, aligning with the biblical prophecy that "Judah is the law giver." He also took on the role of Minister of Education of the Ethiopian government, which, with this being one of my areas of interest, was further affirmation that I was on the right course. Additionally, His Majesty spoke often about the importance of agriculture in the nation's future. Studying His Imperial Majesty has helped me strive to be an exemplar of the King—aligned with how he lived—and to understand that this is the way an upright, righteous man should live. And of course, when you consider him alongside his queen, the Queen of Queens, Empress Menen, you see that perfect balance. So my journey was really rooted in knowledge of self, and that knowledge has guided me ever since. I saw the light of His Majesty. Everything he spoke on has either come to pass or will come to pass. Being able to visit Ethiopia and see the physical structures he built—the infrastructure still in use today—only deepened that truth for me. Ethiopian Airlines, the highest-performing airline in Africa (and, in my opinion, the world), was established by His Majesty. And just as powerful was learning that His Majesty welcomed Africans throughout the diaspora through the Ethiopian World Federation. He invited Black people around the world to help rebuild Ethiopia in the 1930s and 40s after the Italian invasion. Many of us wanted to answer that call, but at that time, the United States denied us the opportunity to support Ethiopia. However, there were a few of us who were able to be volunteer Ethiopians and contribute to the upliftment of Ethiopia. So there are definitely documented accounts from the 30s of people who saw Haile Selassie as a return Messiah. Many of us wanted to support Ethiopia and her cause, and I saw this act as a continuation of that tradition of Africans from the West stretching forth our hands to Ethiopia, and His Imperial Majesty being that God in flesh and that guiding force for how we live, operate, and unify as African people, while at the same time being connected to the global community.

It's really been a practical application of the spiritual knowledge I've learned from His Imperial Majesty—understanding how we can embrace all people, because His Majesty teaches that no one can judge another's faith and that we can all live in harmony. He encourages us to read other ancient scriptures and to honor other faith traditions. His example shows that even in our differences, when we ground ourselves in one love and unity, we can still function as one and support one another. That Ras Tafari way of life has been a guiding force for me—from then until now, and for all the days ahead. One of my closest comrades from my Howard years, and still today, is my good bredren, Kwasi Bonsu. He was an undergrad while I was there, and we both went through our transformation to Ras Tafari together at the Binghi House in D.C., alongside many other brothers and sisters who were students at Howard at that time.

(**Kwasi Bonsu - Friend**) *There was a cosmic shift because there was a Ras Tafari rising up. It was also the time of the Nuwabians, Malachi Z. York, when that movement was popular. It was also the time when the Hebrew Israelites were rising like the Nation of Islam. You name it, it was just a time of Black consciousness. This is the late 90s I'm talking about, and on Howard's campus, we used to have debates. We would hold court on campus, and there might be 20 to 50 people, women and men, and we'd just be debating about anything from theology to politics. These debates were epic. And we burned herb, too. We "legalized" herb on Howard's campus during that time. Those were very fun days, looking back on it, it's almost surreal. Being on the university campus, nobody bothered us, not the faculty, not security, because we were constructive, we weren't causing any problems. We would just be having these lively debates. It was this time that I was introduced to the Nyahbinghi house. The Nyahbinghi house was where I first encountered who would become one of my closest bredren, Cashawn Myers, also known as Binghi Shawn.*

I graduated from Howard with my Master's in Education, with an emphasis on Curriculum Development, in 2000. Upon graduating, I had been feeling a pull to return to Georgia, specifically to Atlanta. Although I gained a lot from my time in D.C. I felt a calling to return to the South and build on the foundation that had been laid by my time in both Tallahassee and Washington, D.C.

After graduating, Shevon and I packed up and moved from D.C. to Atlanta. It was early 2001, and things were a lot different from when I last lived in Atlanta in 1994. For one, I was a married man with a son and would soon welcome my second son, Kefentse Nassor Myers. I was in a different space, not just physically, but also mentally and emotionally, than I was when I left. I left as a teenager just existing in this world, and returned as a man on a mission. I returned with responsibilities, and those responsibilities really gave me the focus and drive to do the things that I wanted to do and allowed me to focus on what I needed to focus on. It also presented me an opportunity to engage with the community in Atlanta. I had found a community in D.C.; now it was time to look for my tribe, or my family, in Atlanta.

I was able to connect with the Rastafari community in Atlanta. Some of them I had met in D.C. when we had gatherings there, and many of them came up to fellowship. So that's where I began to spend time, particularly with the Nyahbinghi House. I began to do programs and activities related to Rastafari celebrations and other gatherings. I was finding my tribe. On top of that, the larger Pan-African community, particularly in the West End, was active. We would go to Kwanzaa events, cultural events, Marcus Garvey Day, Malcolm X's birthday, and a lot more. I surrounded myself with people I connected with and those whom I wanted to learn from.

I attended Clark Atlanta University to pursue my Doctorate in Education. Now, at my third HBCU, my area of study was particularly focused on developing an African-centered curriculum for youth and adults. I ended up spending only one year at Clark, but my time there was pivotal because it was there, in one of my educational leadership courses, that one of my professors and I had a critical dialogue around engaging youth, particularly in the community surrounding Clark.

Clark Atlanta University is a part of the Atlanta University Center (also called the AUC), which comprises Morehouse, Spelman, Morris Brown, and the Interdenominational Theological Center. I was inspired to create Pan-African programs for youths in urban settings and in the inner-city because of my family background. Even though I grew up in a loving family—one that was proud to be Black and proud of our lineage—we didn't have the same depth of historical knowledge that I later found in others. And because of that, I didn't want young people to have to wait until their twenties, like I did, to really learn about their history and culture. That inspired me to think, "What can we do for our young people to give them this knowledge early on, so they grow up with that mindset?" The focus would be on who they are as African people—knowing their story, understanding the great work their ancestors accomplished, and realizing that, they too, are capable of even greater achievements. I wanted to make sure that young people could access that knowledge from an early age—to learn, grow, and build on it—because it is something that has often been taken from us. Our ancestors, forefathers and foremothers were disavowed from learning about their story, speaking their language, using the natural drums, and other tools that we used that connected us with our culture. So this was a way for me to reconnect these young people and make sure they knew about their history and culture, and not just the mainstream European history and culture.

After hours of discussing how we could engage the youth in the community, myself, Ras Tarik, and Sister Sherre started a program that we initially called Plant A C.E.A.D., with the acronym standing for Cultural Enrichment and Academic Development. Plant A C.E.A.D. later became the foundation for the Black to Our Roots program.

We launched Plant A C.E.A.D. in the AUC in the summer of 2002. It was during that time that we had the idea and interest that, in addition to teaching youth history and culture, showing videos and reading books, what about also incorporating experiential learning? Experiential learning, where they could actually touch, taste, feel, smell, and use those senses in their educational experience.

During this time, HABESHA was in its early stages. We formally founded the organization on February 4, 2002, with a vision of creating a space centered on Pan-African culture and focused on youth of African ancestry. We didn't have all the details figured out yet, but we knew we wanted to establish an entity, and HABESHA became the name that would carry that mission forward. I love acronyms, so we thought about a few different ones. I had a travel Amharic phrase book, and it had the word "habesha" in it, which translates to "the original people." I loved the way it sounded and went on a mission to find words that would describe the core of what we wanted our organization to be about. We finally landed on "Helping Africa By Establishing Schools at Home and Abroad."

(**Kofi - *Friend***) *We had something called the Healers Garden Club, which grew out of a talk show we did on WRFG 89.3 FM called The Healers. One segment of the show was called The Healers Garden Club, and we even had a soundtrack for it, created by the Sons of Light. "It's the healers you need these days. It's the Healers to light our way, yeah. The whole world is crying out, about to go insane. It's the healers who heal our pain." They did a whole dub plate for us. It was a very powerful time in Atlanta. The Atlanta that we're seeing now, 20-odd years later, it's clear that anything we see in creation is shaped by the predecessors, and there was a lot done in that time to take Atlanta from our old southern town, or even a Black southern town with deep heritage in one sense, to a more international town. And we were part of that process. The Healers and The Healers Garden Club came in through that context.*

By that time, HABESHA had been established. Helping Africa by Establishing Schools at Home and Abroad, the name speaks for itself. So, you can already see that the mindset of the people driving this energy was focused on one thing: how do we educate and how do we establish schools? So we used our radio show as one of the school rooms, and it became very impactful. And based on that impact, the connection we established with the audience, and the feedback we were receiving, we eventually started what's now known as the ORGANIC FEST. We decided that we needed to have a gathering. We were dealing with a concept; now we wanted to actualize it, where people could actually feel it, see it in its fullness, see it in its prime. Again, knowing we're tapping into something, we have a saying in Guyana that says, "fire stick catch quick." So the concept of an old fire stick is like coal. The fire is gone now, but it catches quick because that essence is already there. So that's what we realized with our people in terms of agriculture. We are agricultural people. Some of us became ashamed of that fact because of the oppression that we faced on the land. Grandmama and Grandfather, or uncle and auntie, weren't usually going to sit down at the dinner table on Thanksgiving and say, "Let me tell you, we used to own 500 acres in Mississippi, but Grandpa got run out of town for standing up to a white man." So much of our wealth and legacy was lost. That's what this was all about: reorienting us to a very rich part of our culture. And not just for some kind of old time sake, not just for memory sake, not just for sentiment, but for a functional reason, which is becoming more and more apparent every day. So that's how it started in a nutshell. We wanted to promote self-reliance, especially when it came to food, with agriculture being the foundation of culture. I think this was before Cashawn was chanting it, since he already knew Baba Tarik Oduno when he came down from Washington, from Banneker City, as we say. But most of us hadn't heard that mantra put that way: "There's no culture without agriculture." Bringing that message to the people, that was the mission. And it still is.

HABESHA was initially focused on connecting the youth with the land through agriculture; however, many adults began to express interest in learning to grow their own food as well, so in 2011, we created the HABESHA Works program. This program was a game changer because we not only shared information with adults about growing their own food, we also taught them how to create business and career opportunities in the agriculture industry. HABESHA Gardens became the hub for the program, with the Dunbar Neighborhood Center being used as a classroom when we weren't in the garden. This program has continued to be a success and one of HABESHA's greatest achievements. To date, we have trained over 300 adults in urban agriculture and agribusiness development.

(Mjumbe - *Jegna*) *When I moved back to Atlanta, I took on the responsibility of learning how to grow food naturally without chemicals - pesticides, herbicides, fungicides, etc. Of course, at that time it was not called organic farming or gardening, that name kind of emerged later, but I knew that if that was going to be my responsibility, I'd need to have land. I ended up meeting Cashawn and his compatriots, and they just kind of came through to me. I'm not sure how they ended up coming to me. I think they all knew my son, but they all came together, and we would be here at my place. So I began to mentor them, and I taught them what I knew so that they would not have to relearn and re-experience the same challenges that I'd already gone through.*

We'd work in the garden, doing different kinds of experiments and working on sustainable agricultural techniques and technologies. That's how I came to know Shawn, Cashawn. I had great admiration for Cashawn and for the other young men who were part of the group that I mentored. They were all very intelligent, creative, intense, and just really engaged. I could tell that Cashawn was very intellectual. I almost anticipated and expected him to go far because of his nature, and because of his focus on learning and his clear ability to organize. He was always very inquisitive, but clear-eyed in his inquisitiveness. He wanted information and data, but he wanted the truth, and he always wanted to see the real picture, and then he wanted to take what he assessed, what he thought, and improve on it. If there were flaws and problems in it, he would fix it. All of the young men were college students at the time, but Cashawn just seemed so much more intense and so much more determined to achieve the maximum that he could out of whatever he was learning about his educational achievements. Right from the beginning, he made it clear to me that he was seeking to achieve advanced education. The other guys all wanted to be educated, but not to the same level as Cashawn did. And I think that this is one thing that differentiated and made him kind of stand out from the rest of the group. It was clear that he wanted to go far.

(Khari - Friend) *One of the earliest challenges that we faced was funding. It's only recently, within the past decade or so, that this movement has actually been one that people can make a living off of. In the beginning, we were kind of just making it happen by any means necessary. One thing I quickly noticed about Cashawn was his leadership. Even in this space, which was one of the original parks and gardens that was funded through Park Pride. That was like a big deal when HABESHA actually got the grant to build out this space through Park Pride, because up until that point funding was kind of non-existent. And even after that, it was still very challenging for us to actually get the resources that we needed to build out these spaces as they needed to be built and also to support ourselves.*

Another challenge was actually getting a committed group of people. Early on, you could count the number of us who were actually a part of the work. At that time, there were only a handful of us who were committed to it, not only as a lifestyle but as a career. I remember Cashawn being really frustrated at one point because every Sunday we would come and do a collective work day, and actually getting folks to show up on those Sundays was tough. I think even to this day, getting folks to actually show up to do the work of maintaining and building out the garden is super challenging.

(Semira - Friend) *I clearly remember a pivotal moment in growing the organization. It was probably 2011, and we went on like this kind of fact-finding mission. We went to a few different agricultural conferences in a couple of cities - St. Louis, Chicago. We even spent some time in Milwaukee, looking at the growing power model. Much of what we learned from that experience became deeply embedded in the original design of the HABESHA Works program. So that was important. We had also gotten some small funding to do a pilot program, which was great, but what real-*

ly became a springboard was receiving a $25,000 grant. We got a $25,000 grant. Now, $25,000 is nothing, right, but we were able to take that money and multiply it so many times. And that was really impressive.

People thought we had like a half a million dollar budget. No. We don't have hardly anything. But what we do have is a lot of ambition and a lot of heart to do this, but no money whatsoever. But that grant really was kind of the launching point, because before then, a lot of the work was being self-funded. Cashawn worked at Georgia State at the time and was using his own money to fund what was going on with the organization. There were even times when he used his own financing to pay me, to make sure that I knew that my efforts were not in vain. He wanted me to know that he valued me and my work, and he wasn't going to abuse or take advantage of my skill set. And that was extremely important, because, you know, through all of this, life is still happening, hardships are showing up, and you're trying to build your dreamsand aspirations when you still have to pay the light bill by the end of the week. So having that funding come through led to somewhat of a kick-off series of funding opportunities that came after that. That was a really pivotal time.

I never saw myself being a teacher, and I never saw myself being a farmer, but teaching people how to grow food brought both of those callings together. It let me merge my love for the land with the joy I feel when I'm sharing and passing on knowledge. And that is one of the main motivating factors in why I continue to do the work that I do. I realized that my natural gift for sharing information—being able to teach, motivate, and persuade—fits hand in hand with my love for the land. I enjoy connecting with nature, growing food, and helping people see what's possible. Bringing those two parts of myself together felt like a perfect match. Over the years, I've tried to hone those skills so I can share what I know more effectively and pass on the enthusiasm I have for the land. And that path is what's carried me to where I am today.

It's a blessing to be able to do the things that I love. I'm grateful to have the opportunity to live out my purpose and share with others the joy that I have from connecting with the earth. Sometimes I'll be lying in bed, and it's like I drift into a trance. My mind shifts into a higher frequency, and that's where my deepest meditation happens. Some people need a specific space or posture to meditate, but for me, meditation shows up through movement and action. I find it most naturally when my hands are in the soil. That's where my mind feels open and free, and where I feel connected not just to the terrestrial, but to the celestial. Working in the soil has been a real healing force for me—keeping me grounded, keeping me motivated, and giving me a sense of peace within myself.

(**Charles Greanlea - Friend**) *I believe I first saw Cashawn around the time when I was going to political education meetings with the Feed the People program with Brother Kalonji. Brother Cashawn was at one particular meeting, and maybe a few subsequent meetings as well. This was probably around like 2011, going into 2012.*

I didn't connect with him initially, but I saw him and my first impression of him was that he was a fairly tall brother, but beyond his physical stature, he just had this presence about him, like regal and yet humble at the same time. You could tell he was a serious brother. So, about a few months later, I found out about the HABESHA Works Program, which, unbeknownst to me, was a fairly new program. I think they had maybe just done their first iteration in 2011.

I didn't make the connection at the time that the brother I was seeing at the political education classes was the same brother who was leading HABESHA and facilitating this program. By the time I signed up for the program, they had given me a scholarship, so give thanks. The HABESHA Work class was fun. I enjoyed the class. It was a great program. Although the program was fun, we got along and would joke with each other, the brother made sure that we understood that it's a serious program. That this is nation-building work. So he always had that understanding motivating him and guiding him in terms of how he maneuvered through life. And I'm thankful for that.

MANNERS WILL TAKE YOU PLACES MONEY WON'T

FIRST VISIT TO GHANA

I remember my first visit to Ghana. It was 2003, and Shevon and I were traveling on a buddy pass. For those that don't know, a buddy pass means you're flying standby—you wait until every paying passenger boards, and if there are seats left, they'll let you on. Luckily, we were able to get a buddy pass to fly to Côte d'Ivoire by way of Paris, France. So we flew from Atlanta to Paris, France, on standby. Then, unfortunately, once we got to Paris, we missed our second flight, to Côte d'Ivoire, because the flight was full. So we ended up staying overnight in Paris. Interestingly enough, we were able to go to the Louvre, which is a famous museum that has a lot of stolen African artifacts. So we saw many of the artifacts that were stolen from our ancestors.

We spent a day in Paris at the Louvre, went to the Eiffel Tower, rode the subways in Paris, and then the next day we were able to get on the flight to Côte d'Ivoire. We flew into Côte d'Ivoire on standby, and the plan was to catch a bus the next day from Côte d'Ivoire to Ghana once we arrived, because Côte d'Ivoire borders Ghana. So the next morning we got up and headed to the bus stop to catch the bus. The bus was supposed to leave around 6:30 am, and we got there at like 5:30 am. We were thinking that we're arriving a little early, so we should be good. But man, when we got there at 5:30, there was a line going all around the building. Needless to say, we did not take that bus. It was full.

So we had a choice to make: either stay another day and try to catch the bus the next day, or try to figure out a different way to get to Ghana. We ended up choosing the latter, and that turned into its own adventure. We had all our luggage with us, and at the time, Côte d'Ivoire was in the middle of a civil war. The taxis in Abidjan could only travel within limited zones, a few miles at a time, before handing you off to another driver. So we went through a series of about five drivers. Each time they would drive a certain distance, stop, let us out, and then another set of drivers would come. We would stand there while they argued over who was going to take us. Finally, a decision would be made, and the new driver would take us another distance. We did this probably for about six or seven hours, traveling from Abidjan to the border of Ghana. Once we finally reached the Ghanaian border, we went through immigration, walked to the other side into Ghana, and caught a vehicle headed toward Winneba. Winneba was one of the towns we wanted to reach because it had a College of Education I'd contacted earlier about teaching, after I finished my studies.

We stayed in Winneba overnight. From Winneba, we then traveled to a place called Kitasethe in the Akuapem Mountains, where Ras Ariel hosted and received us. Ras Ariel had moved to Ghana in the late 90s and had created a website for others who wanted to live in Ghana, or at least visit. Interestingly enough, we had reservations booked for a nearby hotel, but by the time we got to our hotel, we had been about four days late, so we lost out on all of our reservations. Fortunately for us, we give thanks to Ras Ariel, because he hosted us and put us up for the two weeks that we were in Ghana. And it was that time that we finalized and prepped out the Black to Our Roots program, with the support of Ras Ariel and others in the area.

Reaching Ghana alone was monumental, but what was even more powerful was the fact that once we arrived, we felt right at home. We knew that we were destined to return, and I give thanks that we were able to return over time through the Black to Our Roots program.

***

Experiencing Africa firsthand deepened the seriousness I already felt about bringing youth to the continent. In fact, a year before Shevon and I made our first trip to Ghana, I'd decided to go to Washington, D.C. to meet with African embassies and talk with them about our vision for bringing middle and high school students to their countries. So during my spring break, I set up meetings with and spoke to representatives of five African Embassies - Ghana, Ethiopia, Tanzania, Kenya, and Zimbabwe, making them aware of our interest in bringing youth to their country to learn the history and experience the culture, and inquiring about what assistance they could offer. Everyone we spoke to was very courteous and supportive, but they didn't have many financial resources. What they did tell us, though, is that if we were able to get to the country, they would do what they could to help support us.

Of the embassies that we visited that year, Ghana had the most promising opportunity to make it happen, and so in July of 2004, we brought our first group of students, five youth and two adults, including myself, to Ghana. And that began the Black to Our Roots program.

(Sean Irving, aka DJ Rebellion - *Friend*) *I heard Cashawn's name before I even moved to Atlanta. My brother was his advisor at GSU. I was doing similar work in Oakland, taking high school students to Ghana, and Cashawn had just started doing that out in Atlanta as well. I think he had done one or two trips before I even got to Atlanta where he took youth to Ghana. So my brother linked us up when I moved to Atlanta in 2005 because it was in 2004 when I did a trip in Oakland. So for me, connecting with Cashawn and HABESHA felt like picking up right where I left off. I was able to jump in HABESHA and keep doing the same work, which is possibly the most fulfilling work I've ever done in my life - taking children to Africa and being able to watch them reconnect with their culture, seeing how they're different when they come back. I feel like in my time, as a youth, I took a couple of cross-country trips on a Greyhound that I feel like changed my life. I can remember just staring out the window of a Greyhound. But to experience Ghana at that age—I can only imagine what it would have unlocked, especially considering how much it's opened my own eyes as an adult. So being able to come to Atlanta, connect with Cashawn and HABESHA, and begin doing that same work for young people was deeply fulfilling.*

I remember my first trip to Ethiopia. Since 2005, we actually had been planning on bringing our youth and traveling to both Ghana and Ethiopia with the Black to Our Roots program. Myself and Ras Tre, a brother whom I had first met in Washington, D.C. at a Ras Tafari gathering who was now living in Ethiopia doing educational filmmaking work, began discussing bringing youth to Ethiopia as well. We began planning it in 2005, but it wasn't until 2012, seven years later, that we organized our first group to travel to Ethiopia and Ghana during that summer. Before we brought any youth, Ras Tre and I traveled to Ethiopia in April 2012 for a reconnaissance trip to map out the logistics. We spent about seven days on the ground, planning and preparing. When I landed in Ethiopia, I was in total amazement. First of all, traveling on Ethiopian Airlines, where you see nothing but Ethiopian pilots, beautiful Ethiopian stewardesses, and landing in the "New Flower," aka Addis Ababa, was such a treat. I felt as if I had gone inside a portal, surrounded by mountains. Then as I went into the airport, I saw nothing but red, gold, and green planes with Ethiopian Airlines and the Lion of Judah emblem on the side. Seeing that gave me chills because I knew that this was something that His Imperial Majesty Emperor Haile Selassie I had started and founded, so it was a joy to come into Addis. As I traveled around Ethiopia and saw Addis Ababa, I was in awe of the infrastructure established by His Majesty that still stood in this royal, ancient city. Knowing the history of Ethiopia—the resilience of its people, their longevity, independence, and the inspiration they have given to others—made it a full-circle moment for me. As a student at FAMU, I first learned of Ethiopia's greatness, and now here I was beholding the greatness in person! It was such a joy. I got a chance to meet with Mama Desta, a Ras Tafari elder originally from Jamaica living in Ethiopia, and Ras Abye, an Ethiopian elder who lived abroad and had returned to Ethiopia to share the rich history of Ethiopia with visitors like myself. These were the boots on the ground people who helped organize our first journey to Ethiopia with the Black to Our Roots program in July of 2012. Landing in the ancient city of Addis Ababa and seeing the great works of His Imperial Majesty Emperor Haile Selassie in person was truly special. It had long been a dream of mine—as a young Ras in Washington, D.C.—to visit Ethiopia, the land of Black-skinned people, and now that dream was coming to life.

Since my awakening as an undergraduate student at FAMU, it had been very important for me to be a part of the reconnecting of African people in the diaspora, particularly in America to the African continent. As many people have said, such as Marcus Garvey and Malcolm X, unless we know our roots, we would never be as fruitful as we can be. Malcolm X also said that you can't hate Africa and not hate yourself. When you love Africa, you will love yourself. People of African descent who live in America have been told to us that Africa wants nothing to do with us, that we should disassociate ourselves with Africa, but in doing that, we're disassociating ourselves with who we are and our full heritage. So as I began to study and learn more, it became my mission to make sure that all people of African descent are aware of their history and their lineage, especially our young people. I think it's critical. Studies have shown that young people who see themselves reflected in the curriculum and who know their history and culture tend to excel academically. Those rooted in a Pan-African perspective develop a stronger outlook on their education, their careers, and life in general. That has always been one of my goals—not just for youth, but for adults as well. Many adults didn't receive this information growing up; they didn't read the books, the movies rarely show it, and the news often ignores it. I aim to share the wonders of Africa—our history, our culture, and the greatness of Mama Africa—so that we can both contribute to and benefit from this knowledge, now and in the future.

Some of my fondest memories come from witnessing the transformation of Black to Our Roots alumni who have traveled to Ethiopia and Ghana. For some, the change is subtle—how they now see themselves or their outlook on life. For others, it's more profound, influencing their career aspirations and interests. Many participants joined Black to Our Roots with little knowledge of Africa, shaped only by what propaganda on TV had shown them. Then they actually come to the continent and experience the culture. They're able to interact with youth their age, see adults work, witness the bustling communities, and see how people, even with limited material resources, value what truly matters:

family, health, and strength; this leaves a lasting impression. It gives them perspective, they're able to reflect and realize that, "hey, I may not have the latest gadget or the latest phone or the latest video game, but I have family, I have health, I have strength. Therefore, I have to be more grateful." Seeing that transformation in the Black to Our Roots youth has been incredibly powerful, and I've witnessed it in adults as well. We've brought participants to the continent ranging from their 30s to even their 60s—many of whom carried a negative image of Africa. They hadn't experienced the beauty of the land, its resources, the richness of the culture, or the warmth and connection of its people. Often they would say, "I saw someone who looks just like my auntie," or "someone who looks like my cousin." They begin to recognize that we are from the same family. It's one blood, a shared ancestry. For me, witnessing these transformations, whether subtle or profound, and seeing people reconnect in both small and significant ways, has been one of my greatest joys: helping our people return and embark on a journey of self-discovery.

Cashawn and Shevon featured in FAMUan Newspaper

Cashawn and Shevon receiving the Malcolm X Award

Cashawn (far left) Chanting During Nyahbinghi Gathering

Cashawn with Dr. Kambon (left) and Dr. Jackson-Lowman receiving an award at FAMU

Cashawn with the Denards at FAMU

Cashawn Teaching Sustainable Seeds at HABESHA Gardens 2006

Cashawn Teaching at Wesley International Academy 2015

Black To Our Roots, Ethiopia 2014

5
EXPANSION
BRIDGING CONTINENTS

PROVERB: A United family eats from the same plate.

MANNERS WILL TAKE YOU PLACES MONEY WON'T

April 15, 2016, I remember it like it was yesterday. Shevon and I had been talking about moving to Ghana for years, trying to figure out the right timing, the right place, the right finances. We wanted everything to line up. By then it had already been a ten-year mission, ever since 2005, that we knew Ghana was where we ultimately wanted to be. But I was still on the fence, especially with another program and another year approaching. Our usual Black to Our Roots program didn't have a cohort at the time, instead we were working with a group in Orlando to bring them to Ghana. We also had some HABESHA Works alumni who were going to be traveling as well.

On this day, I was headed to catch a flight to Detroit, but before I went I had to drop my children, Kamau and Ila, and my niece and nephew, Aaliyah and Jay, off to school. As I'm taking them to school that morning I'm listening to them have a discussion in the back seat about Africa. My children are talking about how they would like to spend their birthdays in Africa and their cousins are saying disparaging things about Africa. My children are defending Africa, saying, "no, that's not what Africa is like." That sparked something in me. By the time I had dropped them off to school I had made the decision that it was time for our family to move. While my children—my two youngest at the time—still held this pure, untainted mindset about Africa, I knew we needed to go then, before the world had a chance to change it. I made the decision in that moment, and as soon as I did, I felt something lift. A burden, a weight, completely released from me. I instantly felt lighter. I immediately called Shevon and said, "hey, baby, it's that time." So between April and when we left in July, the decision was made.

In July 2016, we traveled with the group that was coming, and then Shevon, the family, and I stayed behind.

We ended up staying for six months—from that July until February 2017—and that's when we began building the HABESHA headquarters. After a few years of going back and forth, we decided 2020 would be our final year of traveling back and forth. So we left Ghana for Atlanta in October 2019, planning to return permanently in April 2020. But when COVID hit in early 2020, we chose not to leave, even though our return date was set for April. So from 2020 to 2023, throughout the pandemic, we stayed in Ghana and never came back to America during those three years. Looking back, it was one of the best decisions of my life.

(Mama Afiya Madzimoyo - *Jegna*) *Cashawn first got my attention as part of HABESHA. I would see them at the Malcolm X festival in the park. It seemed like every year they'd be in the same spot, kind of close to the street. They would be showcasing their program to take the students to Africa. And I was just really impressed. I knew some of the students they'd taken already. I knew some of the families. I mean, they were making it happen, and they were young people, and that always gets my attention. So I wanted to support. I really admired how they ran the whole production, because they were going to have to have the trust of parents and work with the parents. And I knew some of the parents who were also working in the program, they were all working to make it happen. Raising money, getting their passports, immunizations, making it happen. I was so impressed by that. So at some point I said, "I want to support y'all." I didn't have the money that I wanted to give, so I offered to support in other ways. And yeah, that's when they first got my attention.*

(Baba Wekesa Madzimoyo - *Jegna*) *Cashawn is a warrior, healer, builder. That is his personality. He will challenge people, policies, and practices. He will take a stand for our people and against whomever. That is a warrior. But being a warrior only describes one aspect of his personality, he is also a healer because he wants us to heal from the wounds of oppression, so that our families and our relationships work. He's a father and a Baba in the traditional African sense, so he's not just talking about his children. He's talking about our children. And knows that sometimes with our children, the healing Baba needs to show up, not the warrior. He's also a builder. And so, in building and in his approach, what he already brought to it was the understanding that we have to know how to build trust where distrust has been intentionally induced—not just hope that because I read a book and you read a book, we're automatically going to trust each other. How do you build trust? How do you earn trust when the whole system has trained us not to trust one another? And so his personality is that of a warrior, healer, builder.*

My time traveling, studying, and living amongst the people of Ghana has definitely had an impact on my perspective. As someone who, although born outside of the African continent, identifies as African, I've gained a deeper understanding of how other people of African ancestry who live outside of Africa identities are shaped by their influences and life experiences. Being able to live and travel to and in Ghana over the past 20 years has shown me how much the American propaganda system has impacted all of us, regardless of whether or not we're conscious of it. I realized how American I was in terms of not only my mannerisms and spoken language but also my thought patterns. And it's taken time for me to unlearn some of the things that I grew up thinking were normal, when in reality they are antithesis of normality.

Being here in Ghana has shown me that because the American psyche is so deeply ingrained within our subconscious, unless we have a concerted effort to reprogram ourselves, we will perpetuate a lot of the same ills. Additionally, the western cultural norms have influenced the African continent through music, media, arts, etc. The media has shaped how Africans view Africans in the diaspora, specifically in America. Therefore it is my opinion that the only way we can truly change that outlook, both theirs and ours, is by being present. We have to be here on the continent so that our brothers and sisters can see us in real life and not just in films, music videos, and on the news. And as Africans in the diaspora, we also have to witness images of our brothers and sisters who are on the African continent living against the stereotype of Africa being this backwards place, being somewhere that we wouldn't want to be. We have to realize that although both the experience in America as Africans and the experience on the continent as Africans are unique, we still share more in common than what separates us. The way we bridge that gap is by coming together and ensuring that we can share our experiences. That we can freely share those things that make us who we are, unique. It is also important that we recognize the things that we have in common are things that we can build on. It's something that I call "Functional Unity," it's a concept that the African Community Centers of Unity and Self-Determination in Atlanta always discussed. I believe that this concept is something that we really can apply throughout Africa and the diaspora. There's also a concept called "Ubuntu" out of South Africa, which translates to, "I am, because we are and we are, because I am." This concept is premised by the fact that we are all connected and our destinies are eternally intertwined, there is no separation between us. Reggae artist Peter Tosh said it best when he said that no matter where you come from, "As long as you're a Black man, you are an African." My perspective has been shaped by living here in Ghana and witnessing the deep, lingering effects of colonialism. In many ways, I believe colonialism has done more lasting harm to our collective psyche than even the kidnapping, trafficking, and enslavement of our ancestors—because during our enslavement, the enemy was visible. Colonialism works through indirect rule, where you often see Black faces carrying out the oppressor's agenda. This is much harder to combat than seeing the white face that's carrying out the agenda. In many ways, the colonial mindset is so deeply embedded, that undoing it will take just as long as it took to become rooted in our consciousness. And the only way we can begin that reprogramming is by coming together—not on American soil, but on our own native soil. That's where the real healing and problem-solving for Africa and her people can happen. Being here in Ghana has given me the determination to make sure that I continue to be that bridge between the diaspora and the continent. My time in Ghana has deepened my understanding of my identity—not only as an African born in the diaspora, but of the shared identity of all Africans born outside the continent. In many ways, we who were born outside Africa often feel homeless, especially in America. We've spent more than 400 years searching for a place that feels like ours. For me, that sense of home was finally found in Ghana.

Making the move to Ghana has shown me that this vision could be actualized. I also knew that I wanted to continue the programs that we started stateside in Ghana. So I give thanks to the team stateside, including Brother Charles, Sister Raina, Masterpeace, Brother Steve, Semira, Mama Lucy, Brother Ed, and others who have made sure HABESHA continued to thrive while I was laying the groundwork for our return to the African continent. I'm also grateful for the chance to partner with other U.S.-based organizations with aligned missions to strengthen the connection to the African continent. One of those partners was the Afrikan Kulch School out of Orlando—big up Mama Alecia, Baba Weedemiah, and Mama Olabisi, who really spearheaded that collaboration. Our work together began when we trained their team on implementing the Black to Our Roots curriculum. They brought their first cohort of young people and adults to Ghana in 2016, returned with another group in 2017, and then brought a combined Ethiopia–Ghana group in 2019, the year the Ghanaian government named "The Year of Return" to mark 400 years since the first documented enslaved Africans were taken to the Americas in 1619.

Even though we weren't running a Black to Our Roots program in Atlanta at the time, partnering with organizations like theirs allowed us to continue impacting youth—training their leaders, hosting their groups in Ghana, and helping them reconnect with their roots in a real and meaningful way.

Cashawn Laying Tiles at HABESHA HQ 2016

Cashawn at Blue Nile Falls, Ethiopia, 2017

Cashawn and Gail in Ghana, 2018

Cashawn walking with lions in Senegal, 2023

6
FRUITION
THE VISION ACTUALIZED

PROVERB: Courage is the fruit of a decision made in the heart.

I can recall being a student in 1997 meeting with my advisor at the time, Dr. Kobi Kambon, and telling him that one day I would be living in Africa building schools and helping the community. That was almost 30 years ago. So the vision has always been there. On top of that, I had literally drawn a picture of a structure that I wanted to build called the Zion Palace. It was a circular structure with an open courtyard. This was sometime in the late nineties when I had the vision of this structure. In a way, I was prophesying what was to come.

As we built programs over the next 20 years—Black to Our Roots, Sustainable Seeds, HABESHA Works, Urban Green Jobs—I always felt their full potential could only be realized on the African continent. KASI, the Kweku Andoh Sustainability Institute, has been a vision and a labor of love since 2004, when we first traveled to Ghana and knew this would one day be our home. The institute is named in honor of the world-renowned Ghanaian ethnobotanist Dr. A. Kweku Andoh, under whom I was blessed to briefly study under before he transitioned to the ancestral realm in 2011. KASI became the space where our vision could finally take physical shape—a place where we could truly implement our programs. And what better location than Liate Wote, surrounded by mountains, lush vegetation, fertile land, beautiful people, and natural resources everywhere you turn. KASI became the culmination of it all. I often say it's the capstone of my personal and professional life's work—building a healing space for African people, a place for teaching, learning, and reconnecting. Bringing it to life felt powerful because it was the realization of a vision conceived decades earlier.

What has been so beautiful about KASI is the fact that we have been able to bring in and employ over 40 young people from the community of Liate Wote, where KASI is built. They've been part of the development process from the very beginning—chiseling rocks, making blocks, hauling sand, digging trenches, laying foundation, harvesting bamboo. And while the community already used many of these same materials to build their own homes and structures, I think we brought a different perspective on how those resources could be used, especially aesthetically. We wanted people to see the beauty in the bamboo, not just its functionality. Building these structures in this community has also had a real impact on the people's psyche. It's given them a sense of pride to have a jewel like KASI in their community. We've been intentional about involving community members, especially the young people, in the work and in the trainings because ultimately, we envision KASI being led and sustained by the youth who come from this particular community.

Our hope is that we are able to elevate the knowledge that many of the residents of the community have, particularly as it pertains to living off the land, whether that's farming or building. There's also the spiritual aspect of knowing that the land is truly a grounding and a healing force for us. Therefore building KASI is not just about creating an Institute, but about changing lives. Through KASI, we're able to impact lives, especially the lives of young people in Liate Wote. We know the ripple effect will continue and the work we are doing will continue to resonate within the community and outside of it. We'll keep drawing on the strength of our ancestors, engaging the youth in the community, and sparking even greater interest among young people across Ghana and the entire African continent in indigenous ways of living.

Although we never knew what it would look like, we always knew that we wanted KASI to be this hub of knowledge and Pan-African thought. We wanted to make sure we were the best possible stewards of our environment—for the sake of Mother Earth—and to stay in tune with all she has given us by nurturing her in return. That balance is at the heart of KASI, and it's what KASI is now beginning to actualize.

Another essential part of KASI's mission was creating a pathway for brothers and sisters who wanted to return home to the African continent. We had seen many people make the journey with sincere intentions, only to face challenges that pushed them to return—not because they wanted to, but because things didn't work out as they hoped. We wanted to build a system of support for those who wished to come back, because there is no precedent for what happened to African people: being kidnapped from their homeland, trafficked to the West, and forced to labor without compensation.

So we set out to create a program that could truly serve as a pipeline for anyone seriously interested in returning. That's how the Bra Fie program was developed.

Bra Fie is from the Akan language, it means "come home." So come home and learn how to live sustainably. Learn the culture and learn the language so that you can truly acclimate on a cultural level. And beyond that, get informed about land access, citizenship, and everything else required to fully reintegrate into Ghanaian society. That's exactly why we created the Bra Fie program.

Our vision for KASI and the work that we do in Ghana is to create a replicable model for the return of people of African descent to the African continent. KASI essentially serves as a model ecosystem, a self-contained, self-revitalizing ecosystem that is fully off-grid and fully sustainable. KASI has become a model that can be replicated—not only across the African continent as a place to receive people, but also throughout the diaspora as a way to prepare and launch them for their return. We would like to see the return of people of African descent to the continent to help build up the future of Africa. KASI is one example of what that can look like. We invite people to come and learn so that they can now be inspired to take what they've learned to their various locations to build community there while also staying connected to the African continent and to what we're doing on it.

We envision KASI models throughout the continent and throughout the diaspora, wherever African people dwell. Ghana is just the first place that we're starting at, but we see this as something that will grow. We want to connect with heads of government and community leaders who have progressive mindsets and are ready to welcome members of the diaspora bringing skills back to Mama Africa. We have people in the diaspora who are eager to return home. We see KASI, and the work we're doing, as the bridge between the two—linking the diaspora with the African continent in a meaningful, sustainable way. So we've developed curriculum and training programs at KASI around solar and around indigenous technology as it relates to herbal medicine, organic agriculture, and building with natural materials like bamboo and other resources that are abundant in Ghana. Of course, that also includes how we eat—our plant-based approach—along with how we use water and our different methods of irrigation. These are all things we share with our people so they can take them as practical skills, learn from them, be inspired, and stay connected to the work. And not just our work, but the work that other brothers and sisters are doing across the continent to build a bridge of healing from the impacts of the transatlantic and Arab human trafficking systems, as well as the ongoing effects of colonialism, neocolonialism, Jim Crow, and all other forms of oppression.

This is the legacy I want to leave—not only for my immediate family, my biological children, and relatives, but for my larger Pan-African family and, ultimately, the global community. It's a legacy of love, a legacy of healing, and a legacy of vision—of being able to dream and then bring those dreams to life. KASI stands as one powerful example of that vision actualized.

(**Kofi - *Friend***) *A primary memory for me is the profound sense of pride and personal connection I felt when I first visited Ghana—witnessing Cashawn's work, seeing the fruits of his hands and the manifestations of his heart come to life. I had never gone to Ghana before and he'd already been there for a while, more family had been there even longer. I just never had the interest in going at first, to be honest with you. But then I went,* *and going to Ghana and seeing my brother and the moves he's making, seeing the Kweku Andoh Sustainability Institute, that was mindblowing. It was just a feeling of pride in seeing your brethren's works do well and prosper.*

I also had a personal connection because during that time my younger brother, my junior brother, sponsored an African ancestry test for us. And it came back a 100% match that my mother's people came from the Yoruba people of Nigeria. On my father's side it's the Bisa people of Burkina Faso, a mix of Burkina Faso, Togo, and Northern Ghana.

I was talking to Cashawn earlier today and we started talking about one of our nieces that went to Ghana. She's someone we've seen grow up from a baby and how she was so excited to visit Liate Wote. She came back saying, "Baba Kofi, I did this, did this, did this, stuff I never do in America, you know, eating straight from the ground and drink the river water and all this kind of stuff." I'm like, yo, man, that has at least a little bit to do with the space that Cashawn has created, as well as just the beauty of that space. So it was a personal connection. I really felt like I touched an ancient part of my story, being in those mountains.

One of the things that I'm most proud of is having children. I'm grateful that I've had six children and I'm blessed to be a father, it's one of my greatest joys. Being able to leave a legacy that builds upon the foundations laid by those who came before me—my parents, grandparents, great-grandparents, and even the ancient ancestors I may never have known—I strive to continue standing on their shoulders. My family has been my protection over the years because they gave me the responsibility of having to think before I act rather than being so impulsive, because what I did and do doesn't just affect me. My family helps me stay centered and focused and mindful of the fact that I'm building for the future. I'm deeply grateful for my family and all they've provided, for how they've consistently shown up for me. There's truly nothing like the love of your children—coming home after a tough day, and seeing their joy the moment they see you, regardless of what happened out in the world. I'm grateful for my family, and for the blessing of raising my children within HABESHA, rather than having to treat it as something separate. They've always been involved—from attending our events and participating in garden programs, to traveling with us on Black to Our Roots journeys.

That's how I saw it, and one of the main reasons is because I studied Ourstory—the lives of Marcus Garvey, Malcolm X, and Dr. King. As great as they were as community leaders, national leaders, and international leaders, I felt there was one area where I wanted to excel in a way they hadn't fully achieved: being a father. And that balance—between leadership and fatherhood—is no easy task. When you're giving so much of your energy to the community and to your people, what happens to your children? What happens to your wife? My goal has always been to be intentional about making sure my family was a part of whatever I was doing. And the only way I know to do both work for my community and my people and be there for my children is to have my children right there with me. That doesn't mean that there weren't many nights that I spent away from them, however I tried to make sure I included my family in everything that I did as much as I could. Balancing that with fatherhood and being a husband wasn't easy. In my younger years, I was definitely out of balance. I poured myself into the community, holding onto the hope and prayer that by putting in this work upfront, I would create the space on the back end to truly be present with my family. I'm grateful that now, in my later years, I can dedicate real time to my loved ones. I'm still busy, of course, but because I did the work early and have always involved my family in everything I do, I can be fully present with them.

(**Kwasi - Friend**) *He was the first of our circle of bredren that had a child. So he influenced us in just knowing how serious that responsibility is, how real it is, and what that looks like, maintaining a queen and being accountable. You got to go home at a certain point because you have responsibility. I think that's one of the reasons that we bonded, because I was that same person, but I might leave because I got class in the morning or I got a test,* and he got to leave because you have a youth. You know what I mean? So we bonded over understanding the seriousness of the responsibility of being a father, of knowing that you have to provide, you have to go above and beyond, sometimes forgoing even the pleasures of sleep. It's a great sacrifice for your family.

(**Dedan - Friend**) *I have a son who's nine, and I remember when Cashawn had his sons, I think at this time it was just Kidane and Kefentse, and coming out to the garden. Seeing him move as a young father was really cool. I'm more like an uncle to his kids, even to the point where I'll see Kidane on social media now and I'm able to just be like, "Hey, what's up nephew?" So it really was good to see somebody I grew up with really taking on the responsibility to be a father, to be a husband, and to be a community leader consistently. And to put his family first. To put his purpose as one with raising his family. That was a real good example for me and I know for others because we need more of that. We need to see that. We need to see it in action. We need to see fathers, we need to see husbands. We need to see sons and brothers so that we can repair our communities. So that's always been something that I looked at and admired about him.*

One of my biggest inspirations is the revered ancestor, Nana Harriet Tubman, and the work that she did through the Underground Railroad. I see this work that I'm doing with KASI, building these bridges between the diaspora in Africa, in the same spirit as the Underground Railroad. I'm bringing our people home to freedom. I want to leave a legacy of giving everything I could for my people, of honoring those who came before me. And in doing so, I've worked to set up the next generation for success—to live fully and proudly as African people should. I love the symbol of "SANKOFA". The bird of SANKOFA represents the past, present, and future within one space. Always reflecting on the past and honoring what has come before, living fully in the present to move wisely in the now, drawing on the wisdom of our ancestors, and preparing for the generations yet to come. I give thanks for the opportunity to be here in Ghana, living out my vision and my dreams, but also knowing that I really couldn't have done it without all those who came before me - the Baby Roses's, the Kippy's, the Grandma Annie's, the uncle Bruz, the R.C.'s, the Granddaddy Ralph's, the grandma Eunice's, the Duckies - I wouldn't be here without them, all of those who poured into me. The legacy that I want to leave is that I've represented them well. I've made them proud. That they're proud to say that I'm their son, I'm their cousin, I'm their grandson, I'm their nephew, and that I also can create a path for my children to be able to live their dreams, visions, passions.

(Kidane - Eldest Son) *I'm the eldest of my dad's six. I learned a lot about being the man that I am today from seeing the man that he is. A character, that's my dad. You know, it took me a long time to really accept the fact that my dad is cool. It's so weird to say that because he's like twice my age, but he's really one of the coolest guys I know. He's always been that for me. He's always been a role model. He's just so smooth. Honestly, I hate bragging about him, but it's true, and I can tell this to his face. He knows it, you know? He grew up telling me like, "yeah, you don't know this yet, but your daddy's cool." I didn't believe him then, but I grew up and was like, "Guess he wasn't lying. This man is kind of cool." He just knows how to set a vibe. He knows how to make people feel good with his words, how he acts, how he dresses, how he approaches people, how he approaches situations. My dad is truly ONE of ONE. I've met a lot of people in my life and I don't know anyone like my dad. He's a man of integrity. He has a really strong moral compass. Growing up I always felt conflicted 'cause I would look at the man my dad is and wonder how do I go from being a kid and a teenager to like, all that he is, you know? And I always grew up just wondering "how did he do it?" Even now I'm still learning about who he is and who he was to kind of put the pieces together, but yeah my dad is just one of a kind honestly.*

(Kefentse - Son) *I learned a lot from being the second son. Growing up It was mostly me or it was me and my brother. We're close in age, he's only maybe two years older than me. So from him I kind of learned what to do and what not to do. So I tried to take the good qualities and all the good things that I've seen him do and instill that into myself. And subconscious-*

ly, some of the bad things I caught on too as well, but that's just a part of growing up with siblings. You tend to stick up for your siblings and just be involved in whatever your siblings do just because of that connection. Once I had younger siblings it made me become a leader. It taught me how to be responsible at a young age because they often trusted us, whenever we would go out or something, to watch them. It taught me how to share and compromise. I learned to see the good in things and not necessarily think about all the bad things that happened.

The best thing about growing up with my dad was definitely the support. Just having that person in your life you can turn to whenever you might go through things, means a lot, and it's like somebody that's been in your shoes and kind of already knows how you are and is able to say, "Okay, I get you and I understand how you're feeling." Because growing up, unless I had a problem that I couldn't handle by myself, I tended to not ask my parents for help because I wanted to figure things out on my own. And having an older brother, anything I didn't learn from him, if I asked them about it, would usually be things he hadn't done or seen himself. So I kind of just followed and listened to the people that I watched around me, like my parents. So that kind of created a guideline on how I wanted my life to go. So it was definitely impactful, being able to watch my dad and see the kind of man he is. I definitely do appreciate him being there and taking care of me and my siblings.

(**Kamau - Son**) Something that my dad taught me that I will never forget is how to treat others and how to show kindness to other people, particularly how to show kindness to women, especially Black women. He made sure to instill in me how to treat everyone with kindness and respect, and not look down on other people. And he mainly taught me that when we would be gardening. He would tell me to be careful with the plants, show me how to properly take care of a plant, and how to water a plant. So just showing me how to take care of living things and how to take care of everything and treat everything with respect and with some form of gentleness and kindness, that's one thing that I think I will never forget.

(**Ila - Eldest Daughter**) When it comes to being a daughter - the first *daughter - and a sister, when I was younger, growing up with three older brothers was definitely challenging, but now I appreciate it a lot more because I understand what it means to have three men always there to protect me and just be there for me in certain situations where other people may not be. Being the first daughter, I definitely think I'm a daddy's girl, for sure. My dad was always the person I would run to if I had an accident or something, and I would be like, "Oh, kiss my cut," and all of that. Being a first daughter definitely does come with a lot of responsibility as well, just in terms of helping out with things around the house and stuff.*

I definitely got spoiled a little bit when I was younger. I still get a little bit spoiled now, but Ishara has taken a little bit of that away. But I definitely was spoiled when I was younger, and it was nice.

Sometimes the responsibility of being the eldest daughter can be a lot. I feel like I have a lot to prove to myself and to my parents. I feel like my dad has high expectations for all of his children, but I think especially for me because I'm the first girl. But overtime I've kind of learned to accept the pressure and embrace it, and just convert the feeling into really motivating myself and focusing on succeeding, like how he wants me to.

KASI Campus in Progress, 2019

Cashawn and the KASI Domes

Cashawn and Shevon Receive Ghanaian Citizenship, December 2022

Cashawn and His Crown in Full Glory

KASI Campus Complete 2025

7
SUCCESSION
LEGACY & FUTURE

PROVERB: The best way to predict the future is to create it.

When you look at where the work is going—creating more spaces, passing the torch, we truly believe in that vision. That's why I strive to ensure that members of the HABESHA family network always have opportunities to grow, sustain, and step into leadership. This is ongoing work, something we can now pass on to the next generation. Whether it's Ghanaian youth locally or brothers and sisters in the diaspora who join the HABESHA family, our goal is to empower them and strengthen this legacy. Passing the torch and planning for succession has always been central to what we do. My role is to create protocols and practices that can be replicated across the diaspora, so African people everywhere can benefit and continue the work.

(Teena - Cousin) When we were children I didn't consciously know the visionary that Cashawn would be, because we're young, we're playing. But what I did notice in my early 20s, when I realized that he had gone down the path of Ras Tafari, was the fact that he was leading the way, a different way for our family. I realized it even more in 2013 when I came to Atlanta and I was able to live with him, see how he moved within the family, see how he moved within the larger community, the natural leader that he is and how people really look up to him and how in our family, through our bloodline, he is a leader.

Bearing witness to his legacy is divine. I'm so proud of him and so grateful for him. Not just for us as his family, but as a collective as African people. I'm so grateful for him and his leadership and he's so down to earth, yet he's so large. There's so many people out here who speak, but he's actually a doer and leading by example. He's just great. But he comes from greatness, because our ancestors are great. There's a story that I read about my great-great-grandfather, which would be Cashawn's great-great-great-grandfather, Andrew Myers. In 1875 or 1876, 11 years after emancipation, he purchased over 200 acres of land. And from those 200 acres of land, they developed and farmed on about 40 acres of land. And when I read that they cleared the land by hand, that showed me sheer determination, will power, and the foresight to say we're gonna do it no matter what. And I see Cashawn in that same light.

(Shareef Shabazz - Friend) *Cashawn has influenced me as a teacher, community leader, a man, and a protector. Even though I'm not a father at the moment, I've been able to see how he handles his children, disciplines his children. I've seen the way he handles different employees and staff. Those things have influenced me because I see that he treats everybody fair. Cashawn is a very fair person. He doesn't want anything to be unfair or too much this way or too much that way. No, everything is usually in the middle, good, straight up, straightforward. He likes everything to be fair. To me, that's a good trait and a good attribute, just to treat everybody like you want to be treated and do good for people. Just always do good for people regardless of the situation. They might do bad for you, but as long as you come and you leave on a good note and you are fair, that's all you can ask for, is to be fair.*

(Obadele Kambon - Friend) *There's a proverb in Yoruba that says, "Kakinilu de kotoka banidili," which translates to "to greet someone out in the streets." It's different from joining a person to go to their home.*

There was a time when our families lived together. At the time my family and I were preparing to live on a compound, but our home was not yet ready. So I reached out to Baba Cashawn, and asked if we could stay with them for some time until our place was ready. Of course, he opened up his doors to us. And that's when I really got a chance to get to know him.

Cashawn and I would sometimes be up at night talking for two, three, four hours about community building experiences, the community work that we're doing, the nation building work that we're doing, being fathers - he has six children, I have five children - being husbands. We would just talk about the different work that we're doing, the things I'm doing at the University of Ghana. I think KASI was yet to have their grand opening at that time, but when they did, I was there to pour libation. I remember they had a camping experience that my children attended, and I went with them.

So when our families lived together was when Cashawn and I really got a chance to know each other. It went beyond respecting each other from a distance of knowing, "I know you're doing good work for the Black community and for Black people as a whole," to, "this is a solid brother, this is somebody who is very serious about the work that he's doing and this is somebody who has a high level of integrity." It's one thing to know somebody who you have things in common with ideologically, it's another thing to be able to mutually respect somebody from recognizing that, "this is somebody who's about what he says he's about and who is all in, got skin in the game, and is really serious about doing the work more so than just grabbing any mic that's available to talk about what everybody else in the race needs to do when they themselves aren't doing it." And there's way too much of that going on in the world today.

(**Kwasi Bonsu - *Friend***) I have a show called "Lion Love" where I just talk about love stories, and Cashawn and Shevon's is one of the great love stories. I know because I have a great one myself. Their relationship, I think, has been one of Cashawn's north stars in terms of guiding him, keeping him rooted, and grounded. Shevon is his rock.

When you talk about battlefield tested empresses or queens, Shevon is the example. Beside every great man is a great queen, and Shevon is that. Mama Shevon has a range of skills, she has been the back office for HABESHA, the chief administrator of all of our initiatives. She's the one making sure the I's are dotted and the T's are crossed. She's the one that's calling parents and following up if Binghi Shawn forgets something. She's the one to say Binghi Shawn, pick up that, and don't text and drive. She's that voice in his head that's keeping him on point and tight. We always talk about the importance of having a queen. You can't do the work that we do on the level that we do it without a queen. It's just not going to happen. And all of the bredren I know that are working at the highest level have a queen in their life. Because having a queen allows you to be in two places *at one time. It allows you to meet deadlines or lifelines that you probably couldn't meet otherwise. It gives you someone who has your best interest as their priority, and I don't think a lot of bredren know how important and special that is. When anything great happens to Binghi Shawn, the first person he's going to call is Shevon. Anything bad happen, the first person he's going to call is Shevon. I might be next, but Shevon is going to be first to know. And this is a principle that both of us keep. Anywhere I am, my wife know. Anywhere he go, his wife know. If we go missing, the queen have to know what to do, where the last place to look, how the thing is going to go. We have to think this way because of the type of work we're doing, we can't be naive to say that there might not be opposition to this liberation work.*

So their relationship was an example to me. My wife and I were together in high school, so when I reflected and I realized that this was a very solid sister, let me rally forward, that was one of the great decisions I made because, again, seeing how Binghi Shawn was working with his queen, my queen worked similar with I. Meaning that even right now, the home front I know is secure. I don't have to have sleepless nights.

Same with Mama Shevon. And she knows every facet of HABESHA because she's been there. When there was no money and we were just making things happen, she was there staying up all night to make sorrel or a pint up of ginger juice. One of the main things we used to do with HABESHA is make juices and bakes and all of that. And the one who took that up when the staff was gone was Mama Shevon. So every part, from preparing food for events to modeling in the fashion show. She is exemplary in terms of being willing to fit in everywhere that's needed. I consider her my sister as well and she's close with my queen, so it's just from one bredren to another, I want them to look at their relationship as a possibility of what is possible, you know?

A woman can take your idea and amplify it and make it real, she's Mother Earth.
She has that power of nurturing and manifestation and that is what

Mama Shevon has done. Binghi Shawn would not be able to execute as he does without Mama Shevon.

Mama Shevon is that check and balance for the bredren . I'm also one of those check and balance for the bredren, but Mama Shevon is the chief in terms of everything got to go through Mama Shevon, so you already know when you bring it it better be good.

I think their relationship is an example for all bredren. And I think historically it will be just like a Marcus Garvey and a Amy Jakes Garvey. Just like how we look at his Majesty and Empress Menen. When we tell the story of Binghi Shawn, we'll have to leave a large portion of that story to Mama Shevon.

***

I've been fortunate enough to have people around me, especially men, who have been able to live their own lives on their own terms. It's helped my view of success to grow and evolve, starting at the foundational level. To me, success has always meant having control over my own time. I can remember my granddaddy Kippy, for as long as I've known him he always worked for himself. He was a businessman. So all my life I knew that I wanted to work for myself, not for anyone else. Even if I had to temporarily work for someone, my goal was always to be able to work for myself and to employ others. Success for me is being able to provide for myself while also creating opportunities for others to live their best life in their purpose and passion. It was never about monetary gain nor fame, it's always been about the impact that I can make on current and future generations. That's how I measure success, and how I view those who came before me as having achieved it. I see success not just in the present moment, but across generations. A hundred years from now, what will be said about me? Will my name still be called? Will my great grandchildren say, "You know what, he was a great man. He provided a way for us. He gave us an opportunity to fulfill our vision and our mission." If so, that's what I will deem success, and I want to create successors. As the saying goes, "there's no success without successors." I'm here to help the future generations—starting with my own children, but extending to all the children and adults whose lives I've touched over the years. How can I be of benefit to someone else? So many people have poured into me, shaping the man I am today—the village that raised me. Now it's my responsibility to pay it forward through the work I do, whether on the African continent, in North America, the Caribbean, Europe—wherever my feet touch the ground. I want to have a positive impact on our people and support them on their journey of healing and resolution.

Cashawn and Kwasi in Accra

Cashawn and Mama in Atlanta 2025

Cashawn in Reflection at Slave River in Assin Manso, Ghana

Cashawn at the Peak of Afadjato

Cashawn Receiving Award with HABESHA Alumni

The Myers Family

CONCLUSION

I am grateful to everyone who has been a part of my life, whether in big ways or small. My journey is a testament to the value of community, the importance of the village—which we, as African people, truly need. I am also a testament to resilience and possibility: my mother had me at fifteen. I could have been just another statistic, yet she made the choice to stay the course, to nurture me, to raise me, and to support my dreams and visions. For that, I am forever grateful.

My goal is always to make those who poured into me proud. I want them to know that their time wasn't wasted and what they put into me was appreciated and built upon. I want them to be proud to say, "Hey, I had a part in helping that young man be who he is today."

These are the words I share with all of our young people: stay focused on your vision. You may not know everything you want to do right now, but continue to look within and ask yourself the important questions—why did the Most High put me here on this earth? What is my ultimate mission? Whenever you visit a community in Ghana, the king, the father, or the elders will always ask you, "What is your mission?" You can answer in any way you choose, but that question is one I continue to ask myself at every stage of life: what is my mission?

As I enter the 50th chapter of my life, I find myself asking: what is my mission going forward? And I believe my mission now is to help others discover theirs—to empower people to find their purpose. I truly feel that I'm already living my passion and purpose, and I intend to keep doing so. I want to guide others as they navigate life, community, and all the layers of this human experience. My aim is to be a vessel of service, of love, and of inspiration to those around me. I want to leave a legacy that my children, other children, and our people can build upon—a legacy that makes this world better because I contributed to it, just as so many before me have done. That's the legacy I hope to leave.

ACKNOWLEDGEMENTS

I would like to express my deepest gratitude to my family for their unwavering support throughout this journey. To my mother and father, Rita Mitchell and Victor Myers, thank you for showing me the way and never giving up on me. To my siblings, Raymond, Lionel, Gail, Antonio, and Chris, I love you and am proud of you. My wife, Shevon, who has endured my demands for the past 25 years, and my children, Kidane, Kefentse, Kamau, Ila, Kofi, and Ishara, who have inspired me to be the best version of myself for them. To all of my family members who have babysat me, fed me, or just spent time with me, I will never forget you. A special thanks to my writing coach, Summer J. Robinson, for believing in this story and championing it tirelessly. The editorial team at Silver Bangles Productions deserves applause for their insightful feedback and dedication to shaping this manuscript. This book would not be the same without the exceptional cover photos by photographer, Sheree Swann. You have an eye to capture the right moment, for this I say, "Meda ase Pa!" Finally, to the readers who embark on this adventure with me, thank you for giving my story a home in your thoughts.

CASHAWN MYERS

ABOUT THE AUTHOR

Born in a small rural town in Southeast Georgia called Woodbine, Cashawn Myers has taken his life experiences to make a positive impact on the world. He comes from a lineage of farmers and teachers, and as a youth, he was hesitant to follow either of those family traditions. It wasn't until he was a sophomore in college that he wholeheartedly embraced his purpose in life. Mr. Myers is a father of 6, husband, international organizer, farmer, and teacher who received his Bachelor of Science in Psychology from Florida A&M University and a Masters of Education with special interest in Curriculum Development from Howard University. As a founding member of HABESHA (Helping Africa by Establishing Schools at Home and Abroad) Inc., headquartered in Atlanta, GA, Mr. Myers has served as Executive Director since its inception in 2002. HABESHA is a Pan-African organization that cultivates leadership in youth and families through practical experiences in cultural education, sustainable agriculture, entrepreneurship, holistic health, and technology. In 2003, Mr. Myers led the development of the HABESHA Gardens Complex (HGC), a one-acre facility that serves the metro Atlanta area by providing education and training in urban organic agriculture, sustainable energy technology, and green living. HGC also hosts several events, including festivals, concerts, movie nights, and other cultural programs throughout the year. Mr. Myers has been instrumental in establishing training programs in Atlanta for K-12 youth (Sustainable Seeds-2004), young adults (HABESHA Works-2011), and seniors (Golden Growers-2013) around sustainable urban agriculture and healthy living.

To fulfill his passion for connecting youth of African ancestry with their cultural heritage, Mr. Myers created Black to Our Roots (BTOR), a youth leadership and rites of passage program that promotes African cultural values through critical research, community service, and fundraising. This program was specifically designed to reduce the negative impacts of poor education and community apathy that exist in so many urban environments. BTOR culminates in travel-study to Ethiopia and Ghana, providing youth with the tools to become active participants in the unity and development of their local and global African communities. Mr. Myers has led over 200 youth and adults from Atlanta, New York, Detroit, Washington, D.C., and St. Thomas, VI on the "Journey of Self-Discovery" since 2004. In 2007, an award-winning documentary film entitled "Black to Our Roots" was made, which told the story of Myers and the youth of the program.

HABESHA's success has led to the establishment of HABESHA Foundation, an NGO in Ghana, in 2005, and has supported the establishment of 3 schools, 1 orphanage, and 1 clinic in the Eastern and Volta Regions. HABESHA opened the Kweku Andoh Sustainability Institute (KASI) in Liati Wote, Volta Region in 2022. KASI is named in honor of world-renowned Ghanaian ethno-botanist Dr. A. Kweku Andoh. KASI is a marriage between an eco-resort and a research and training institute that highlights instruction in sustainable and renewable eco-holistic practices from an indigenous African perspective. Additionally, KASI serves as the International Headquarters for HABESHA to host individuals and groups for African cultural exchange.

Currently, Mr. Myers lives in Ghana with his wife and 4 children, and resides in the Eastern Region. As a recognized master teacher of 20 years, Mr. Myers has been an invited keynote presenter at regional and national conferences, school systems, colleges, and universities. With a culturally relevant approach to youth development, he is known for his dynamic, interactive presentations for teachers, administrators, parents, and students. HABESHA's success has led to the establishment of affiliate branches in Washington, D.C., Accra, Ghana, and Addis Ababa, Ethiopia. Several universities, community organizations, and institutions of faith have honored Mr. Myers for his work in the upliftment of peoples of African ancestry, particularly youth. The work of the organization has also been featured on television, radio, and print media throughout the U.S., Caribbean, and Africa. Mr. Myers travels extensively throughout Africa, Europe, and the Caribbean, sharing his experience of sustainable agriculture and healthy living.

Connect with the Author:
www.habeshainc.org
IG: @habeshainc | @cashawnmyers | @the_kasinstitute